Enchanted Fairyland Coloring Book

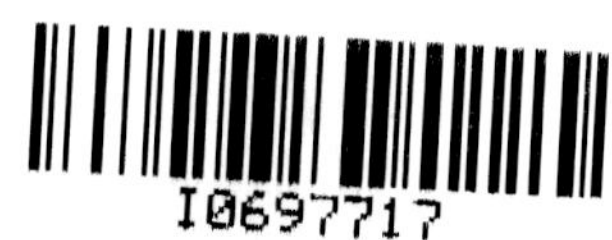

by

Avri Maplewood

Test Color Page

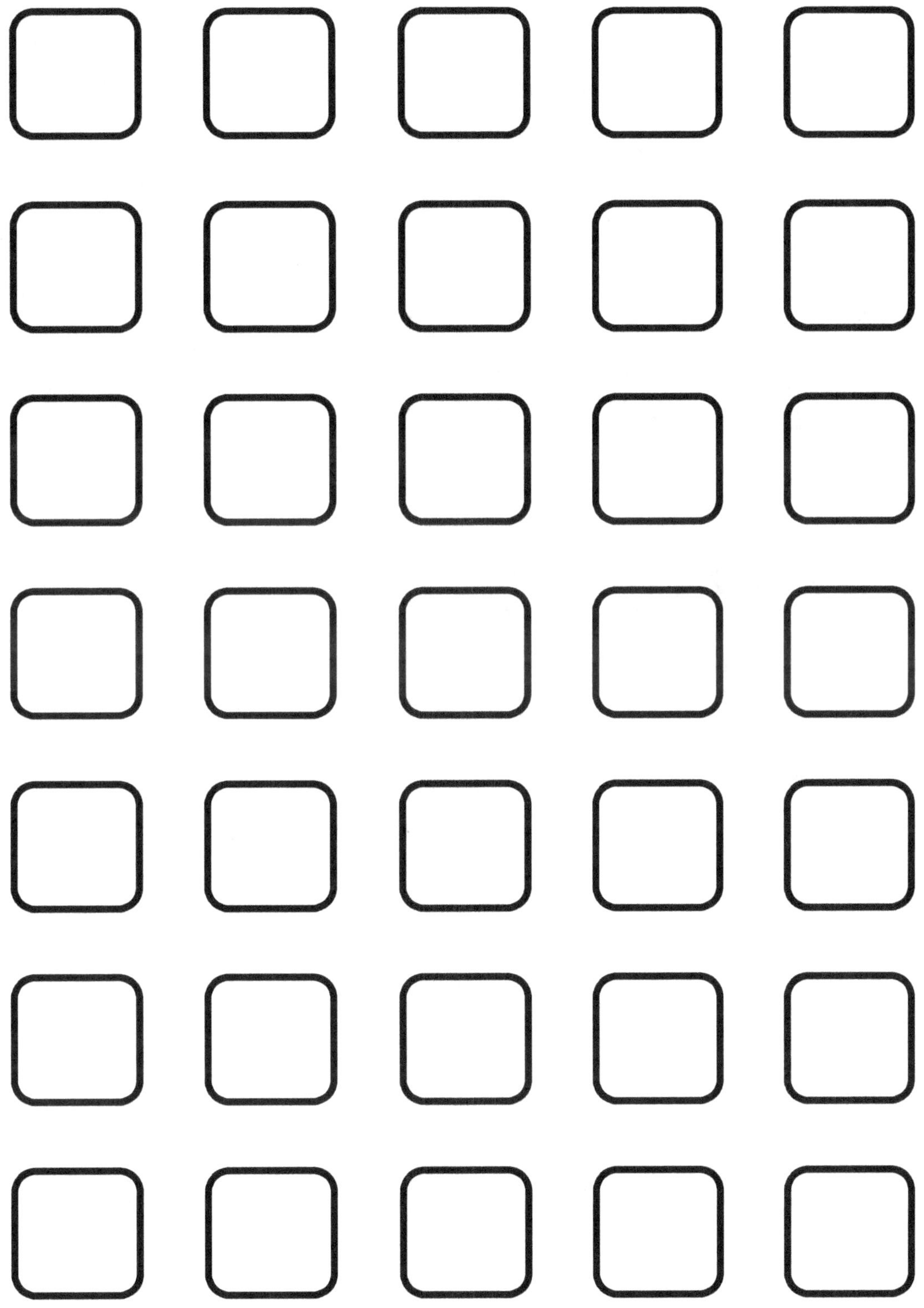

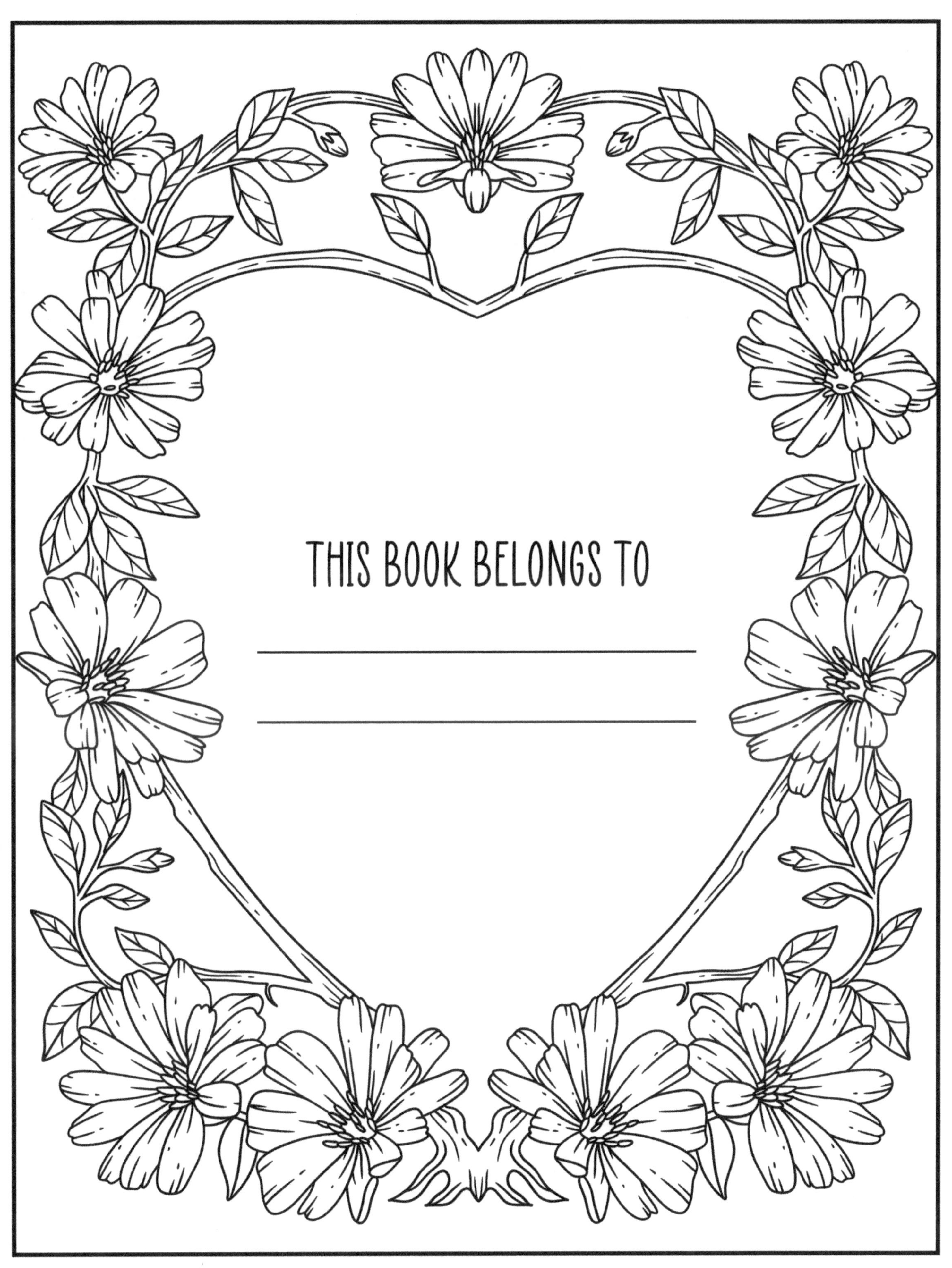
THIS BOOK BELONGS TO

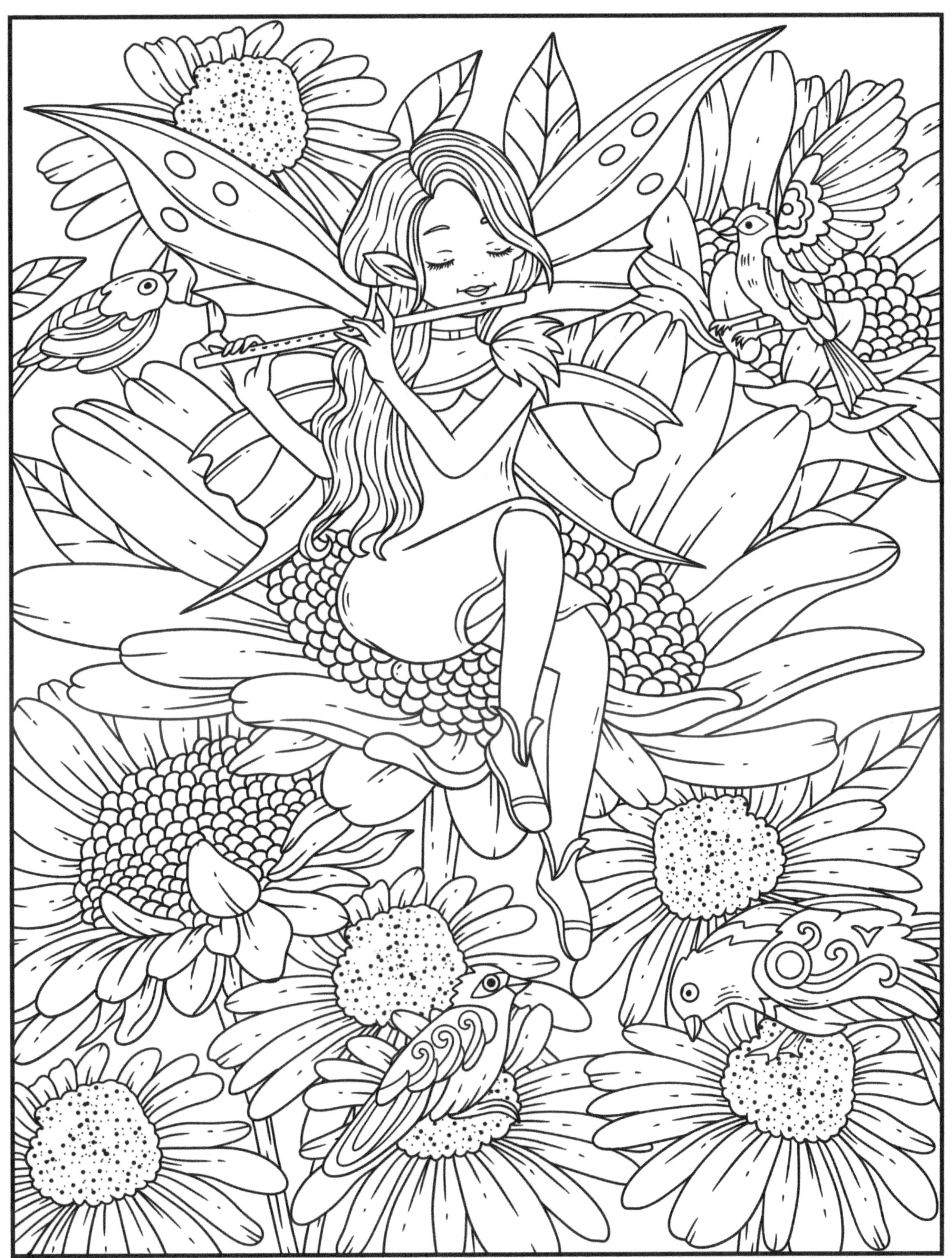

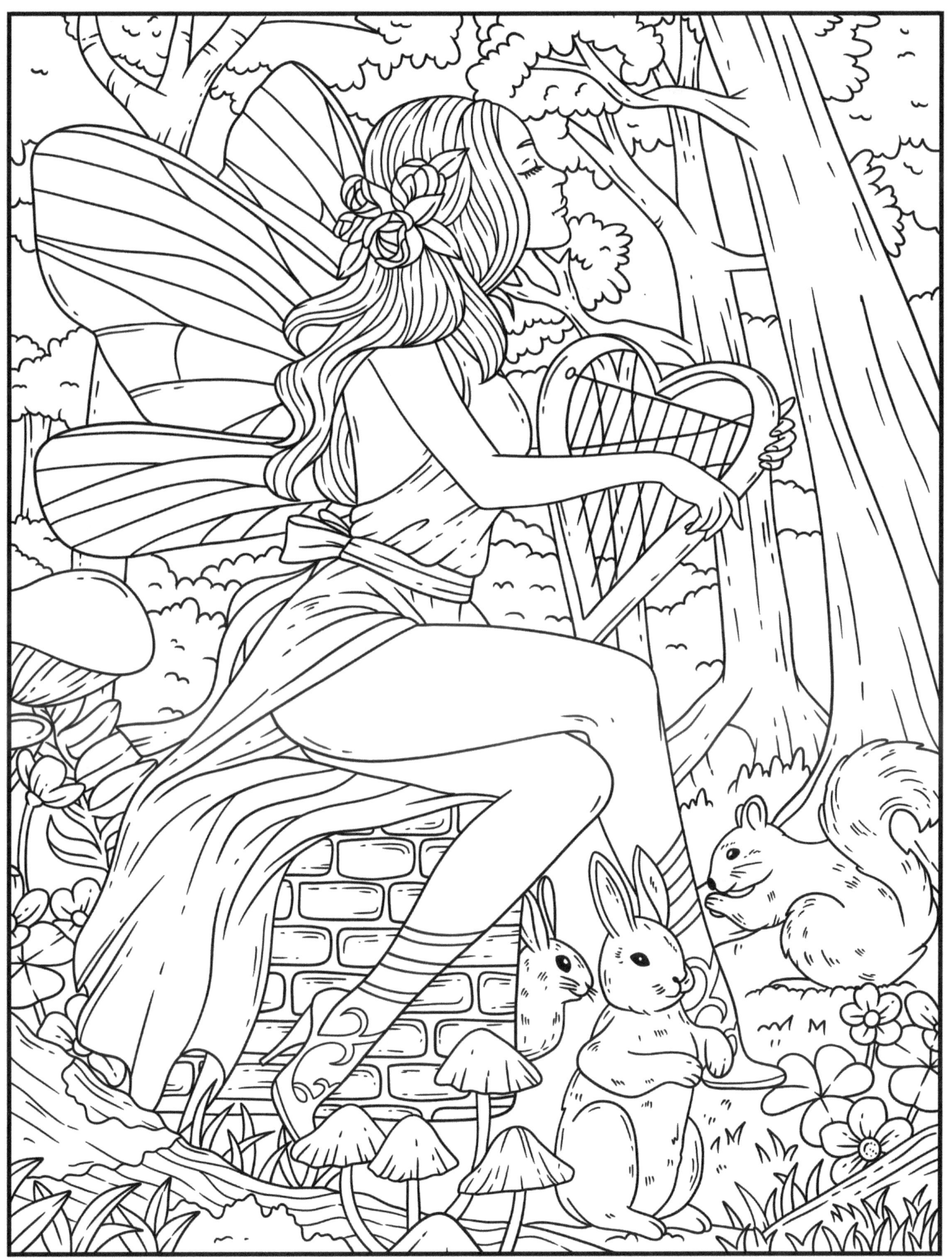

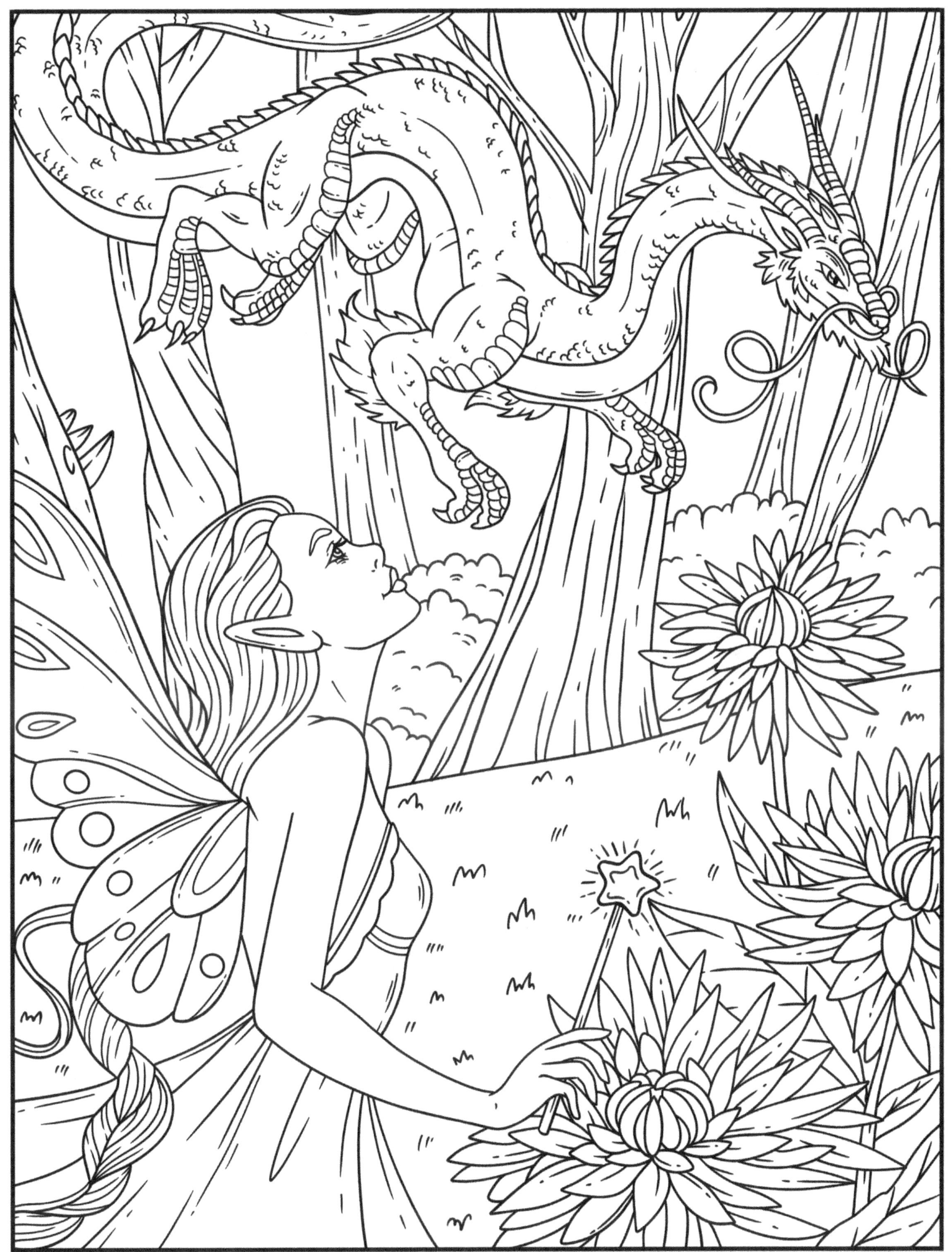

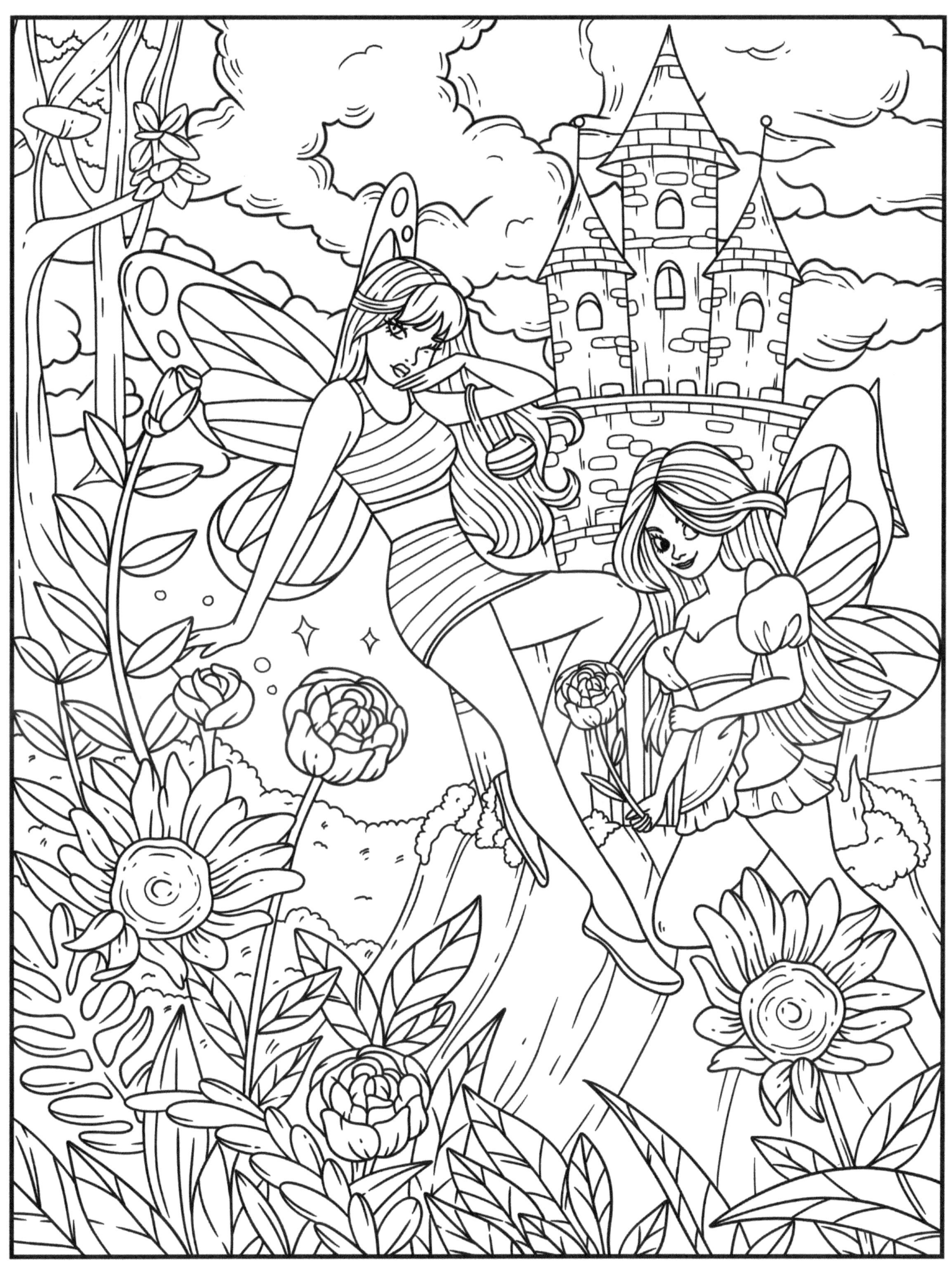

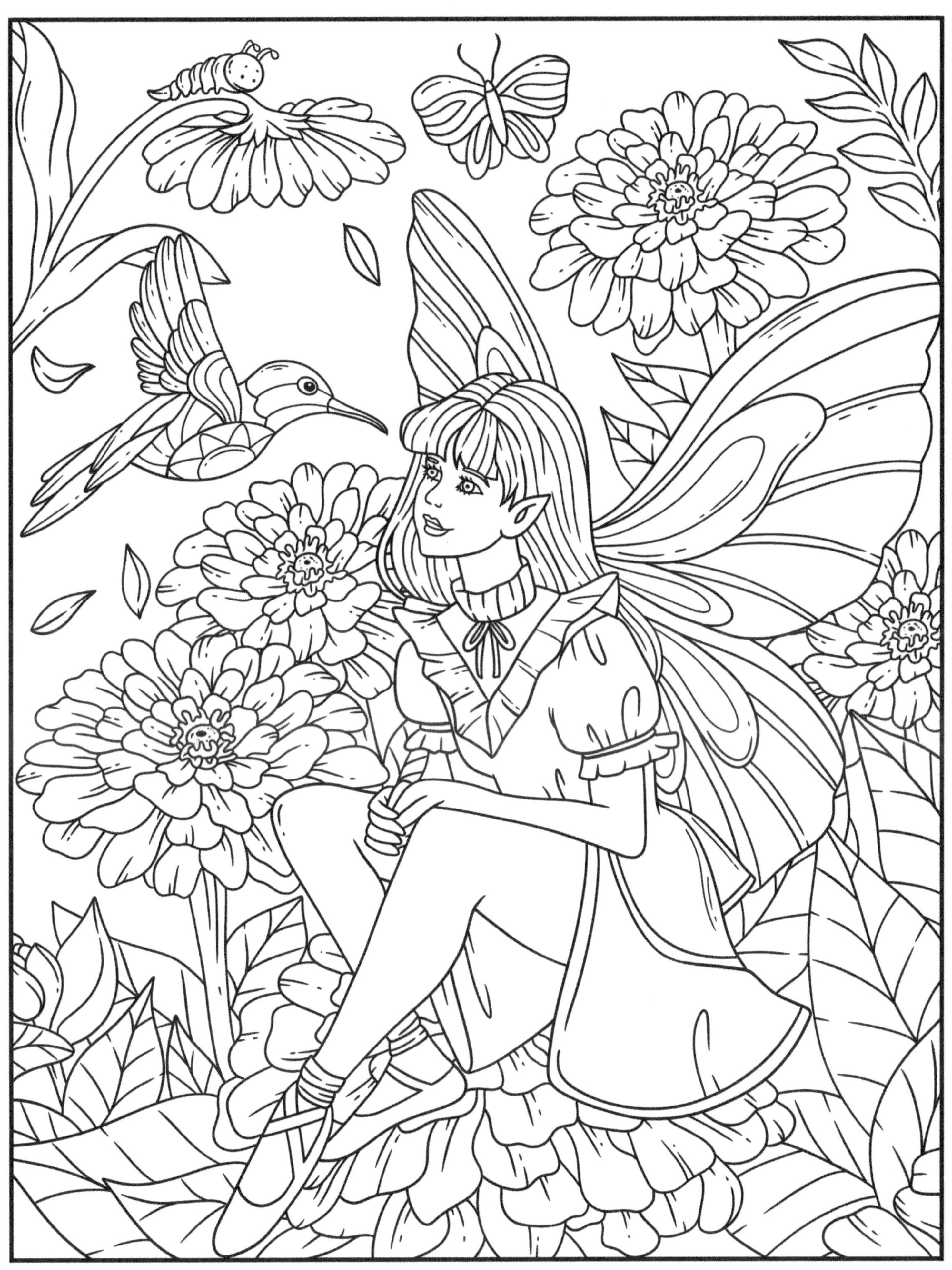

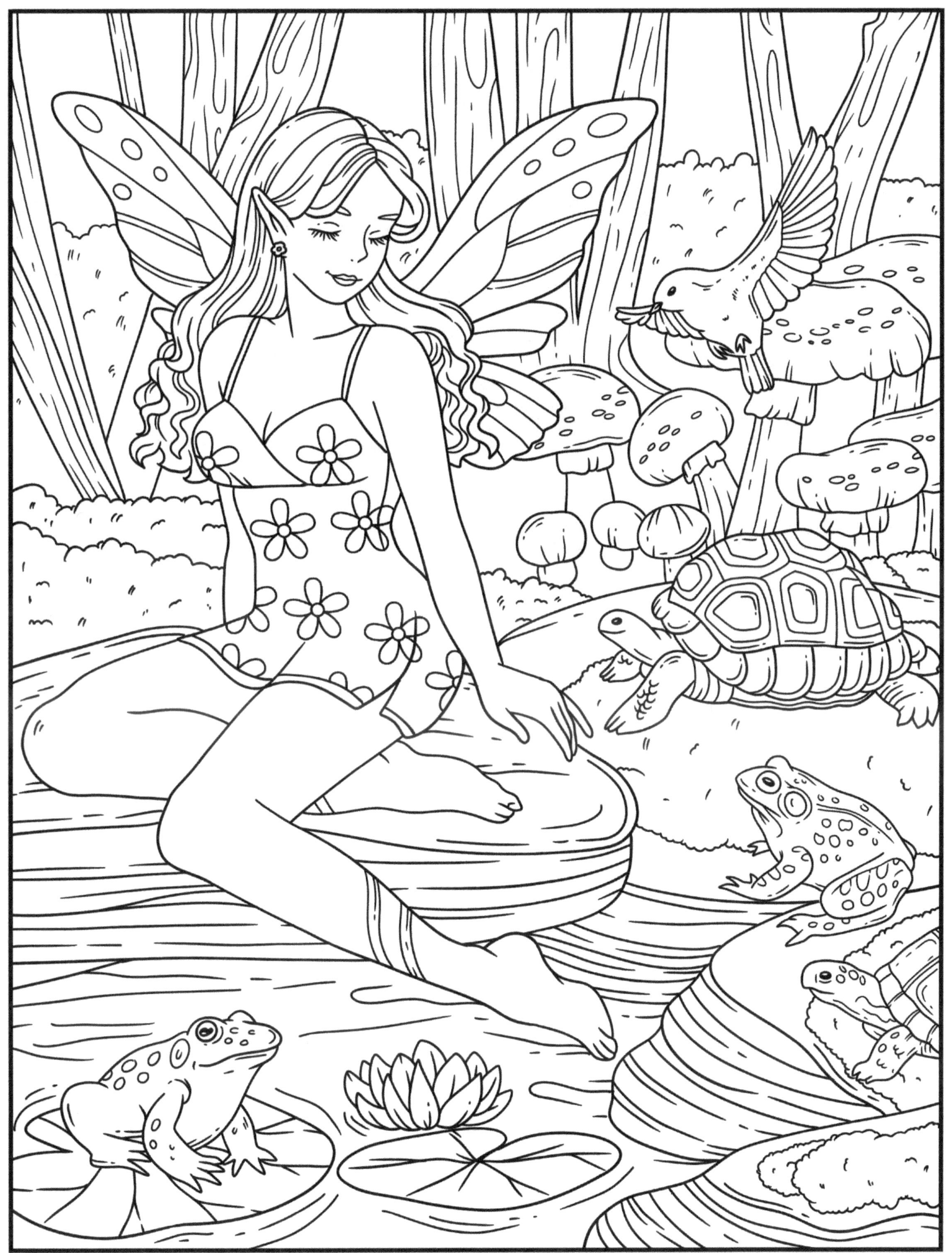

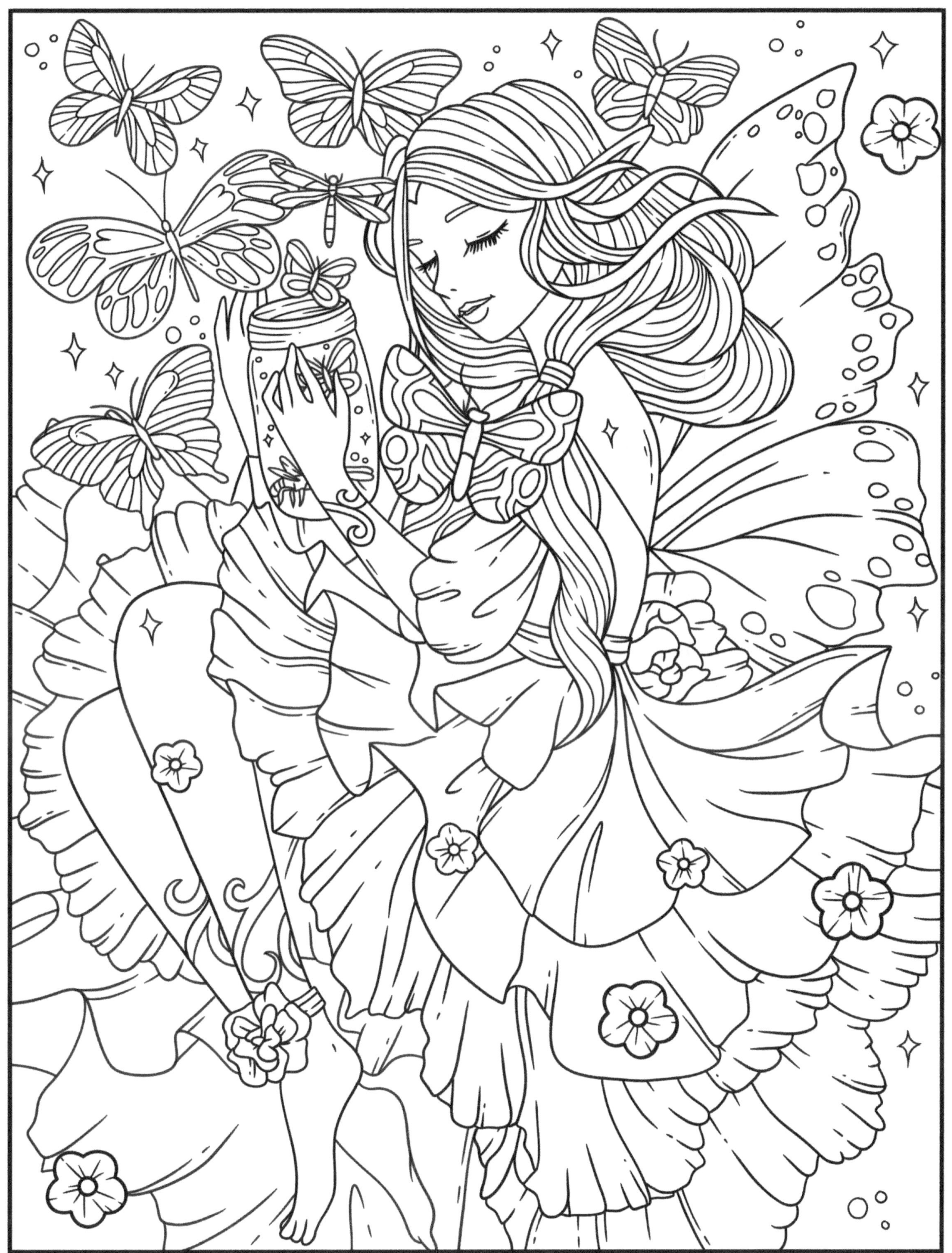

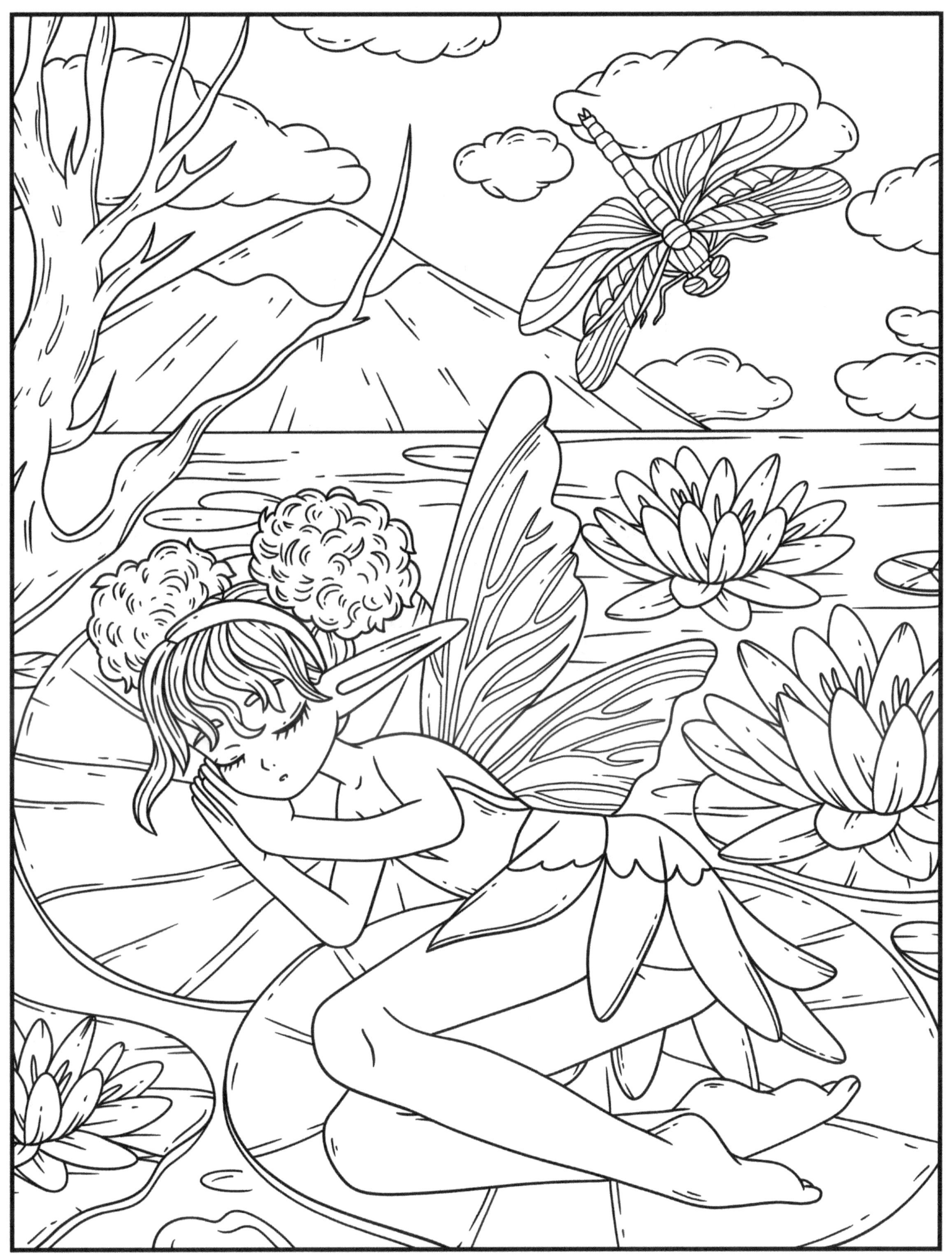

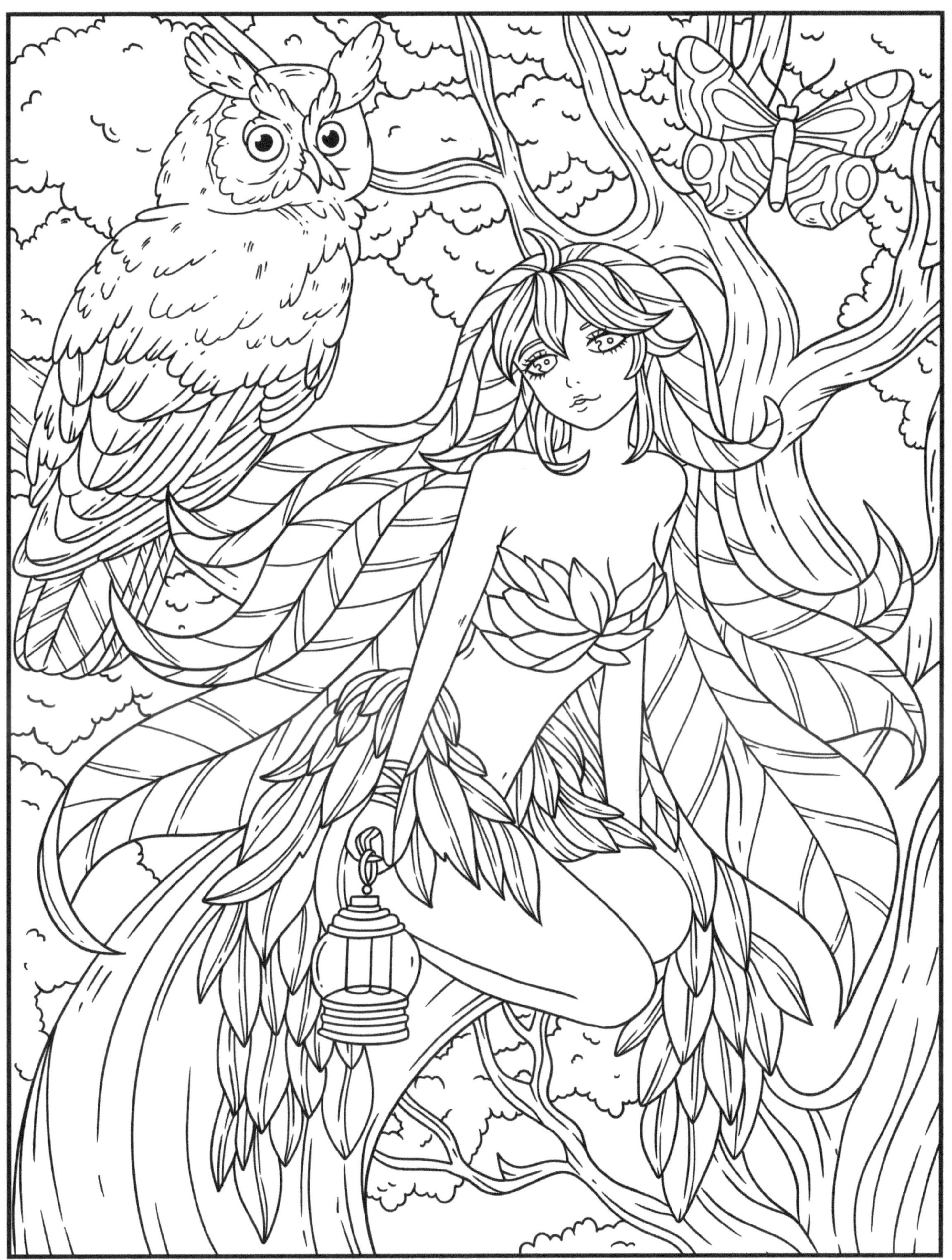

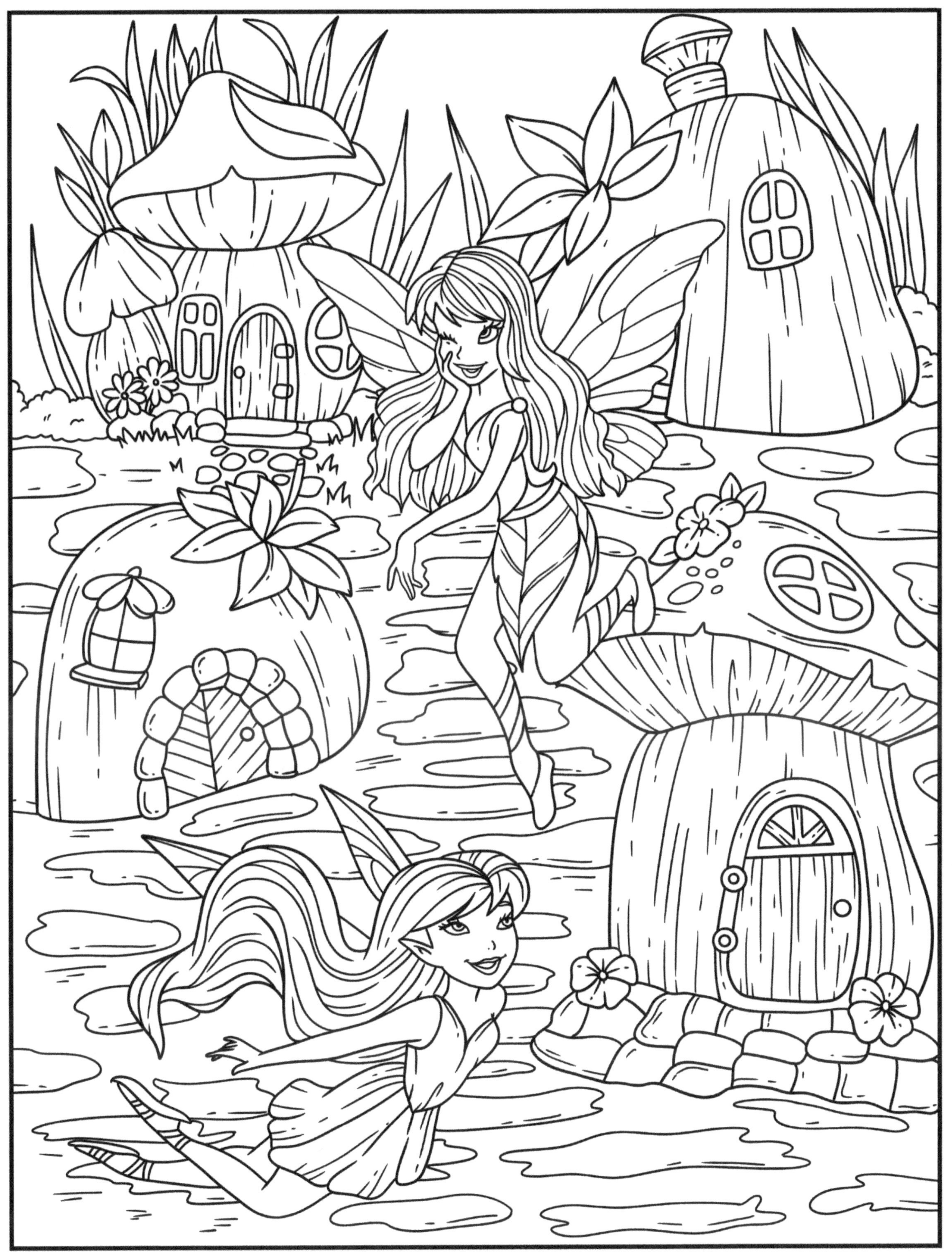

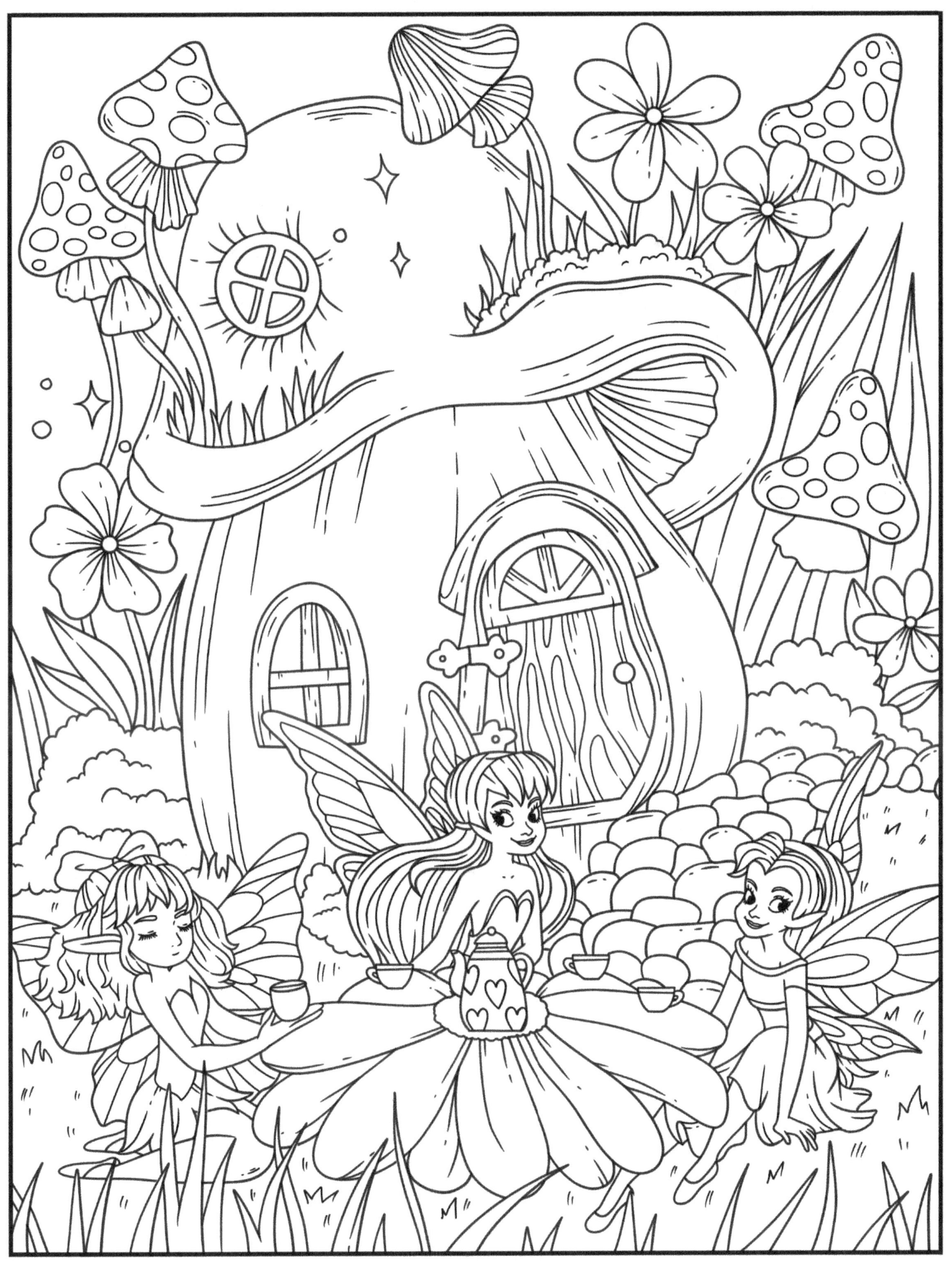

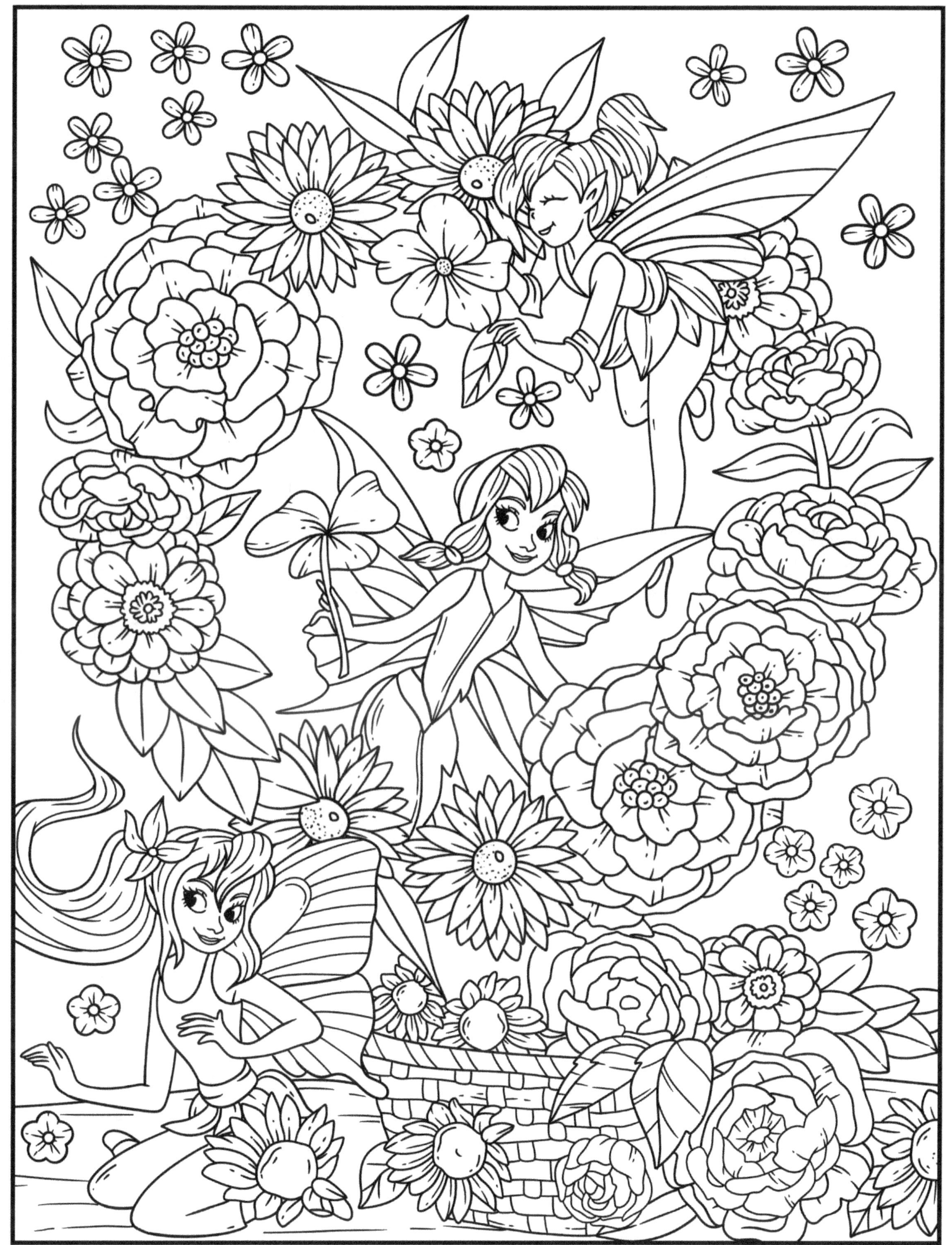

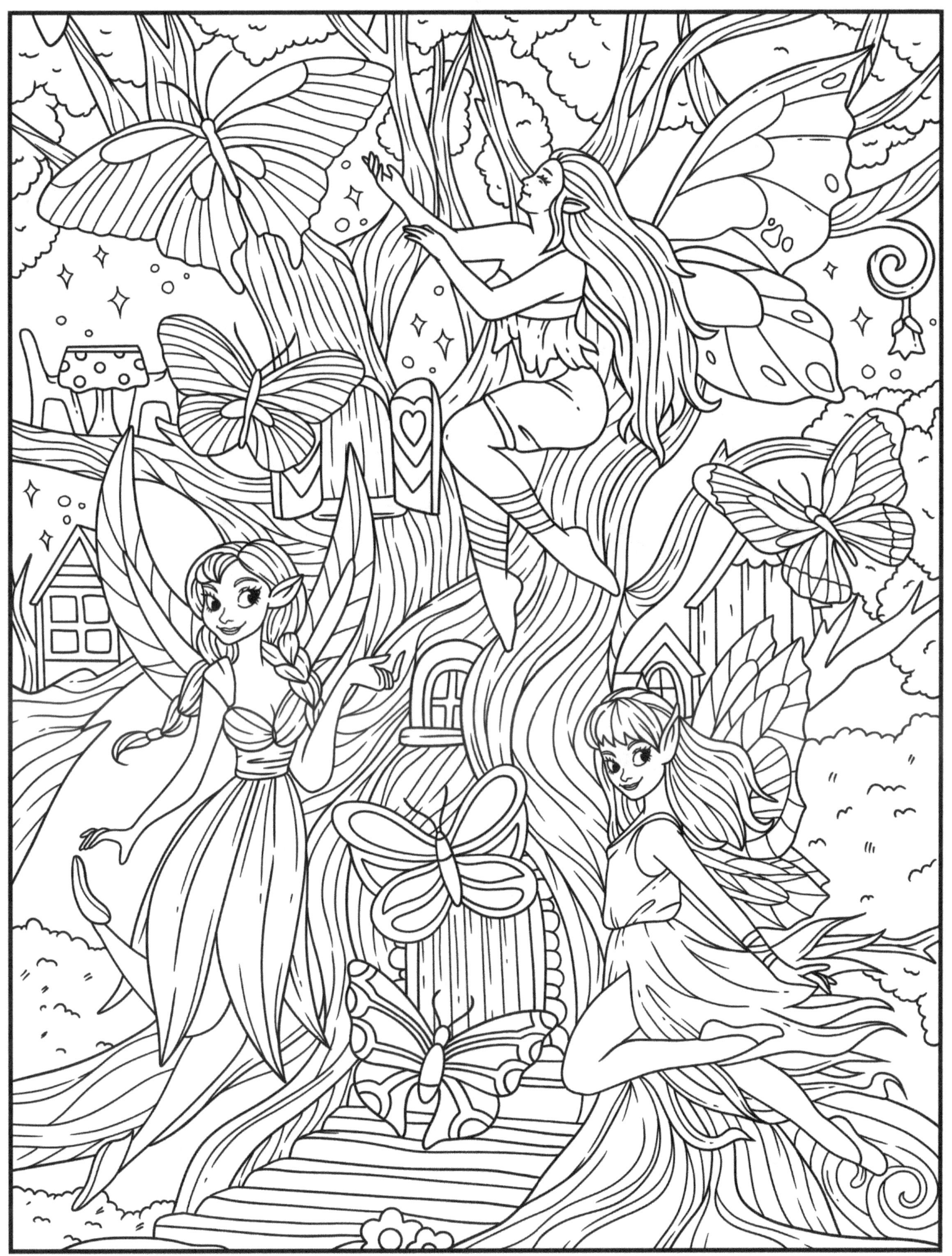

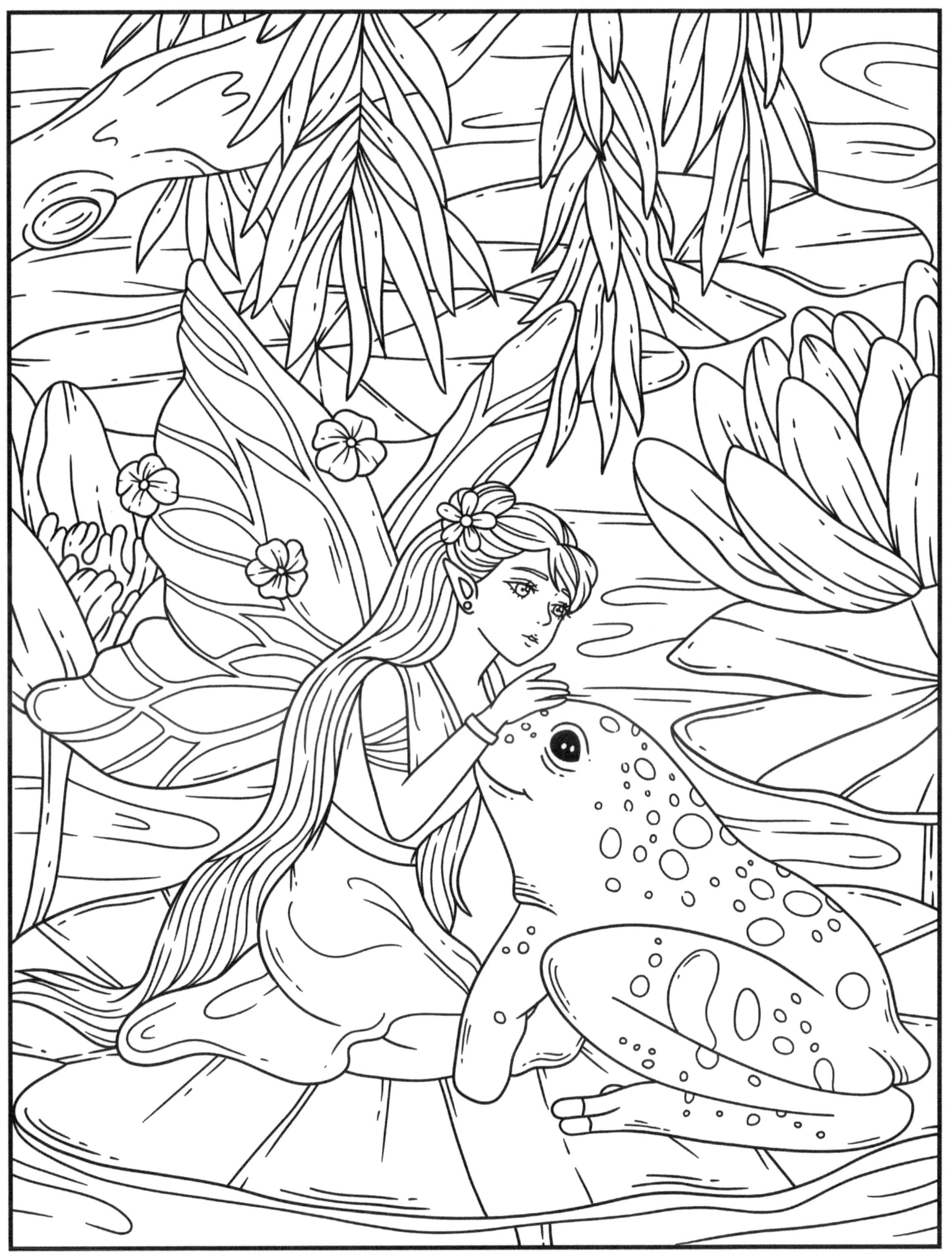

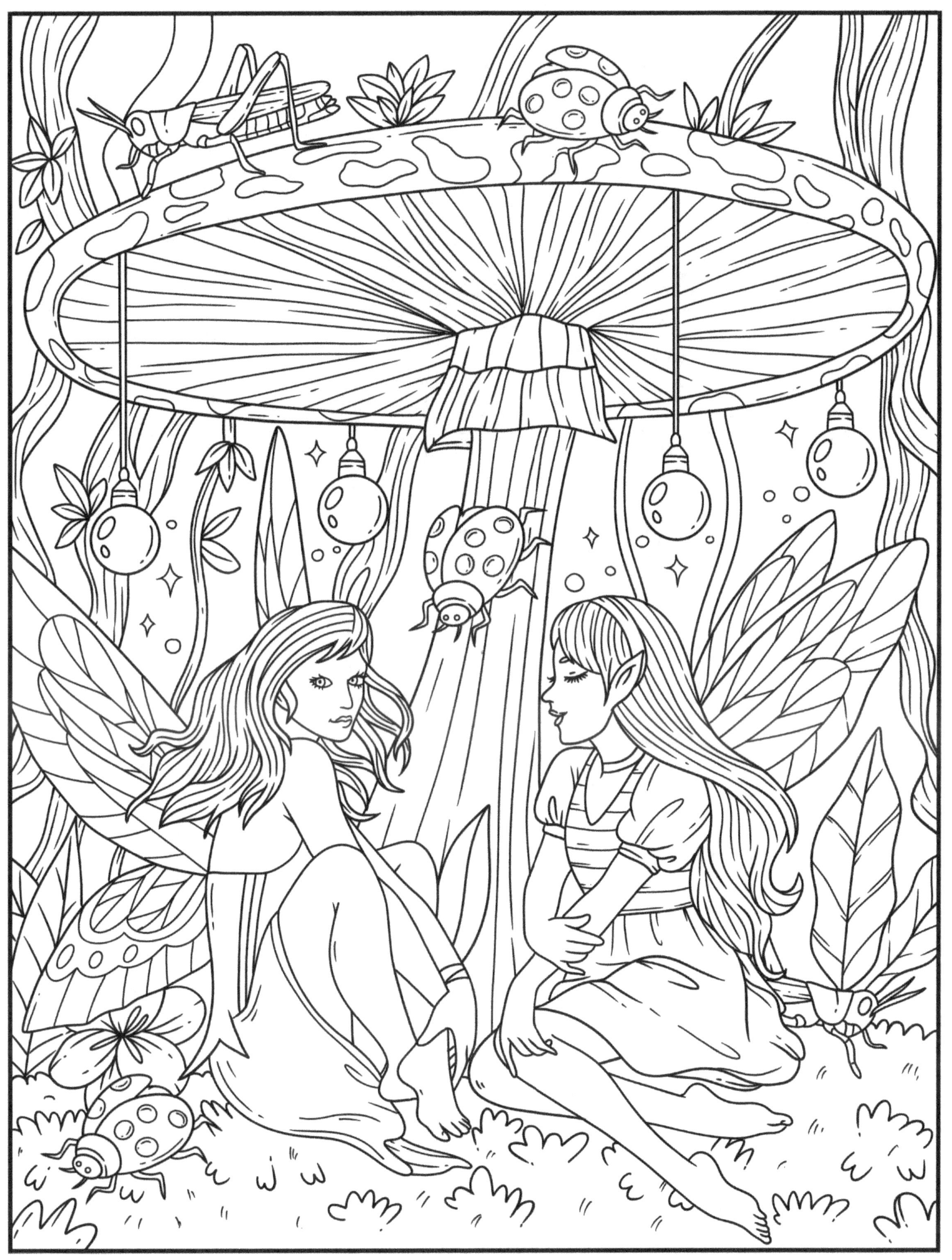

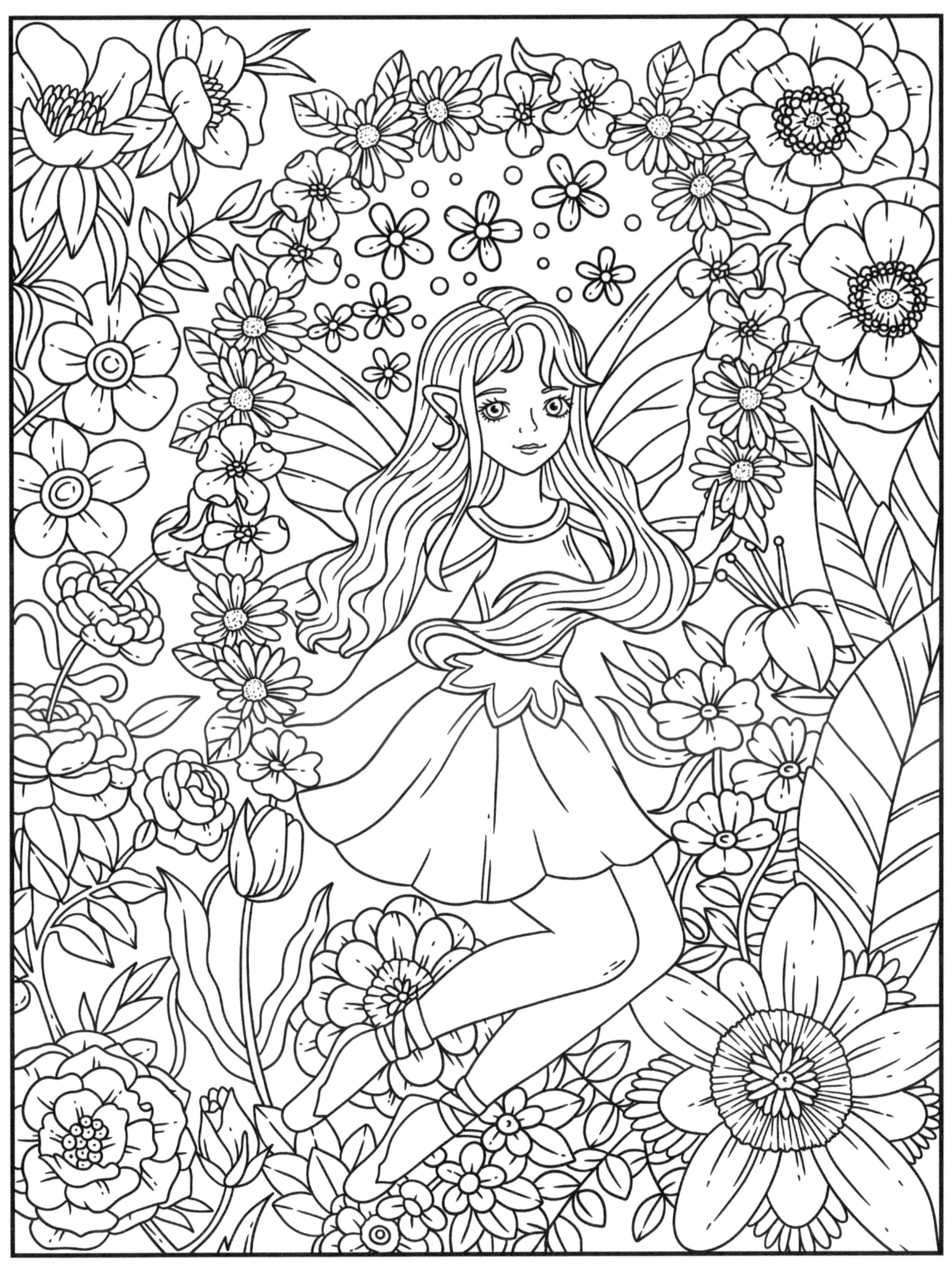

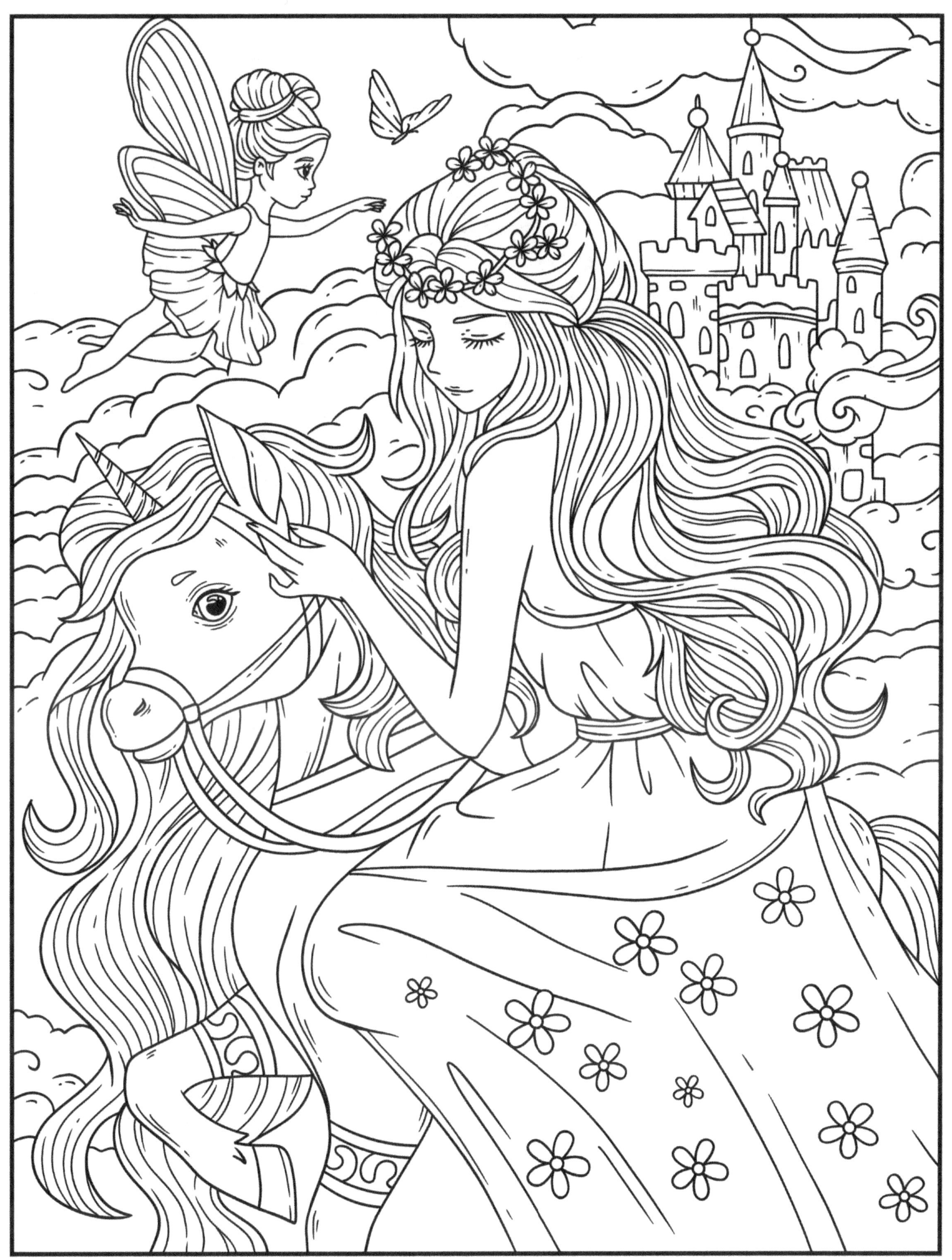

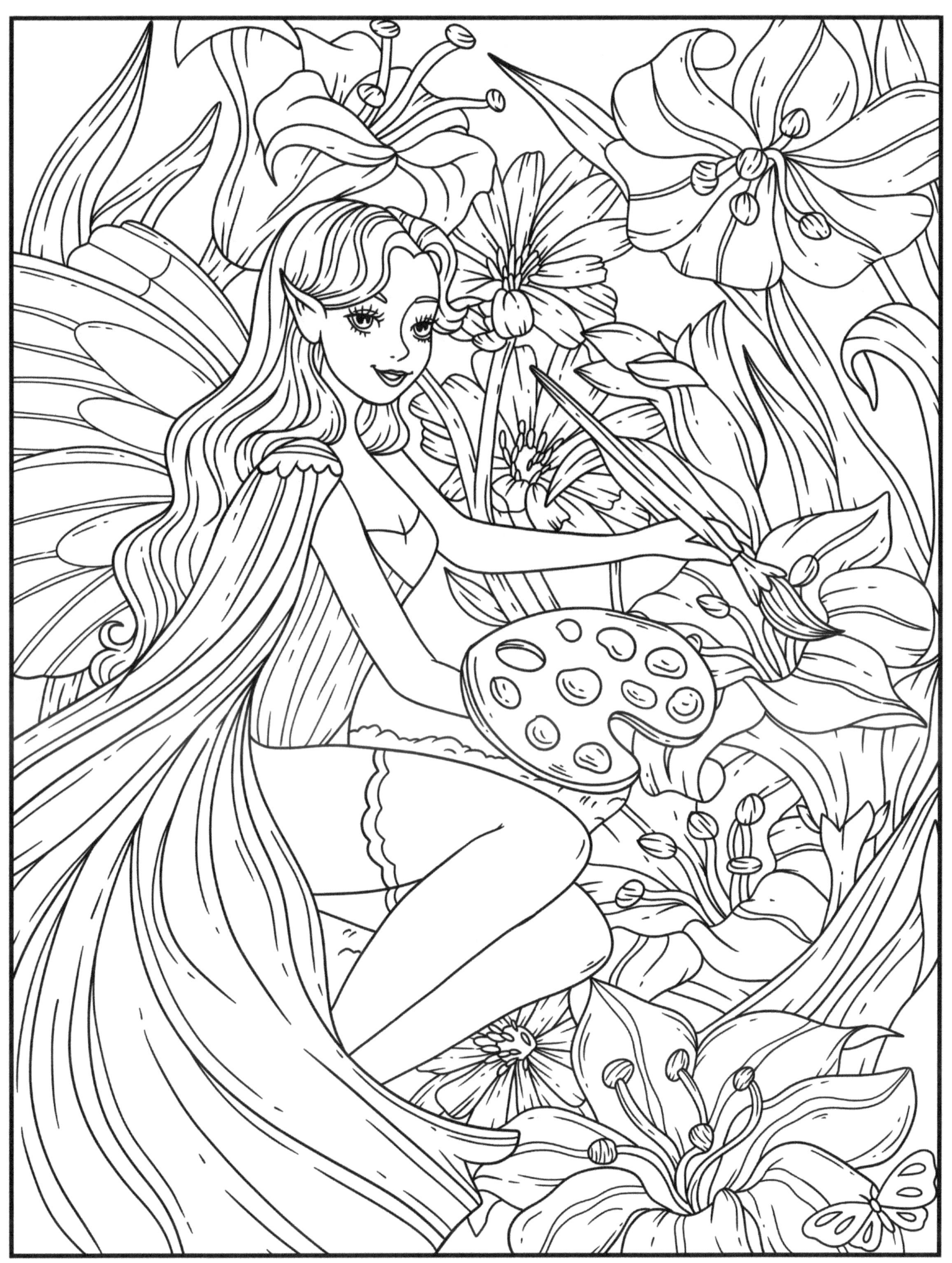

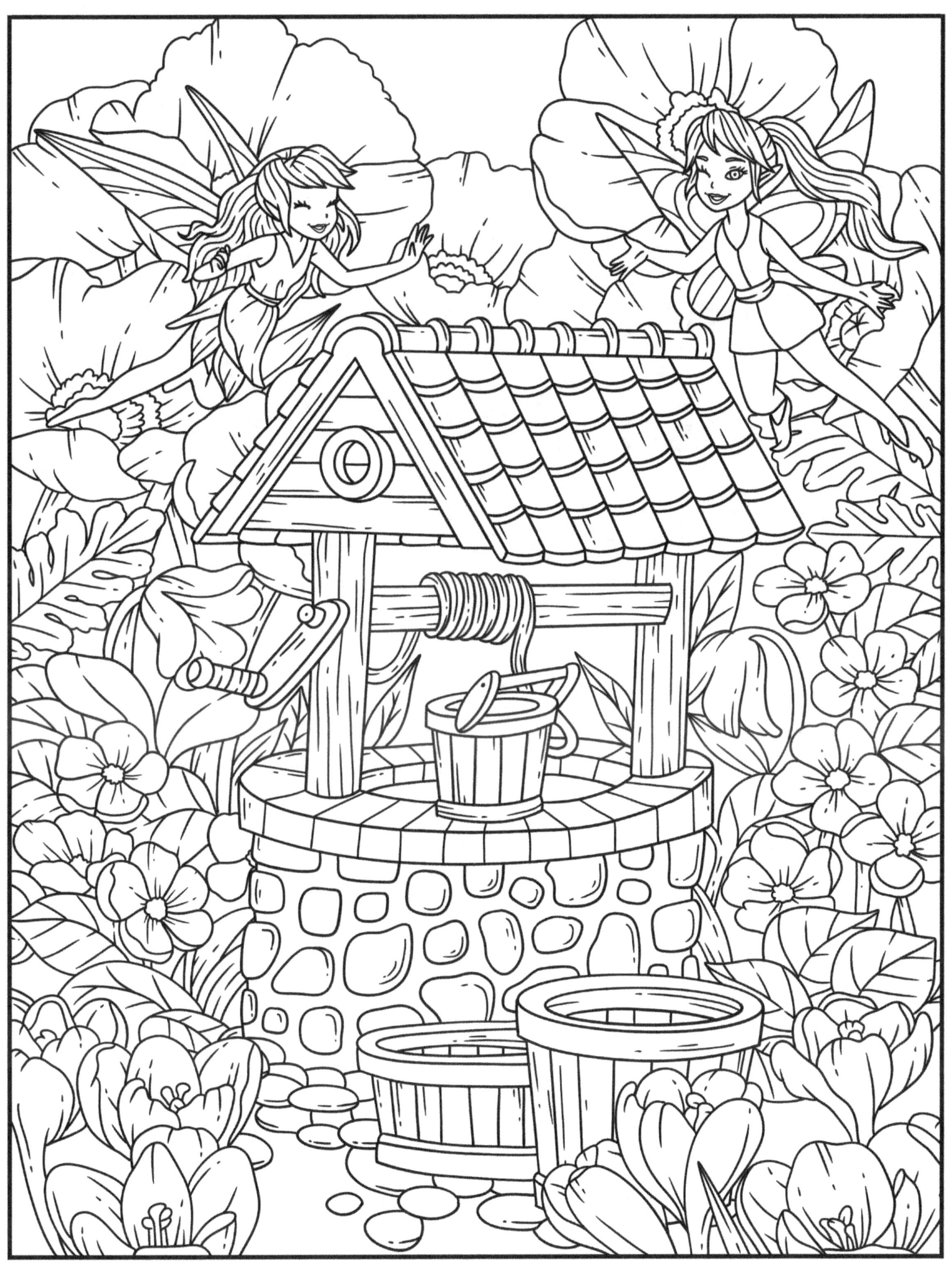

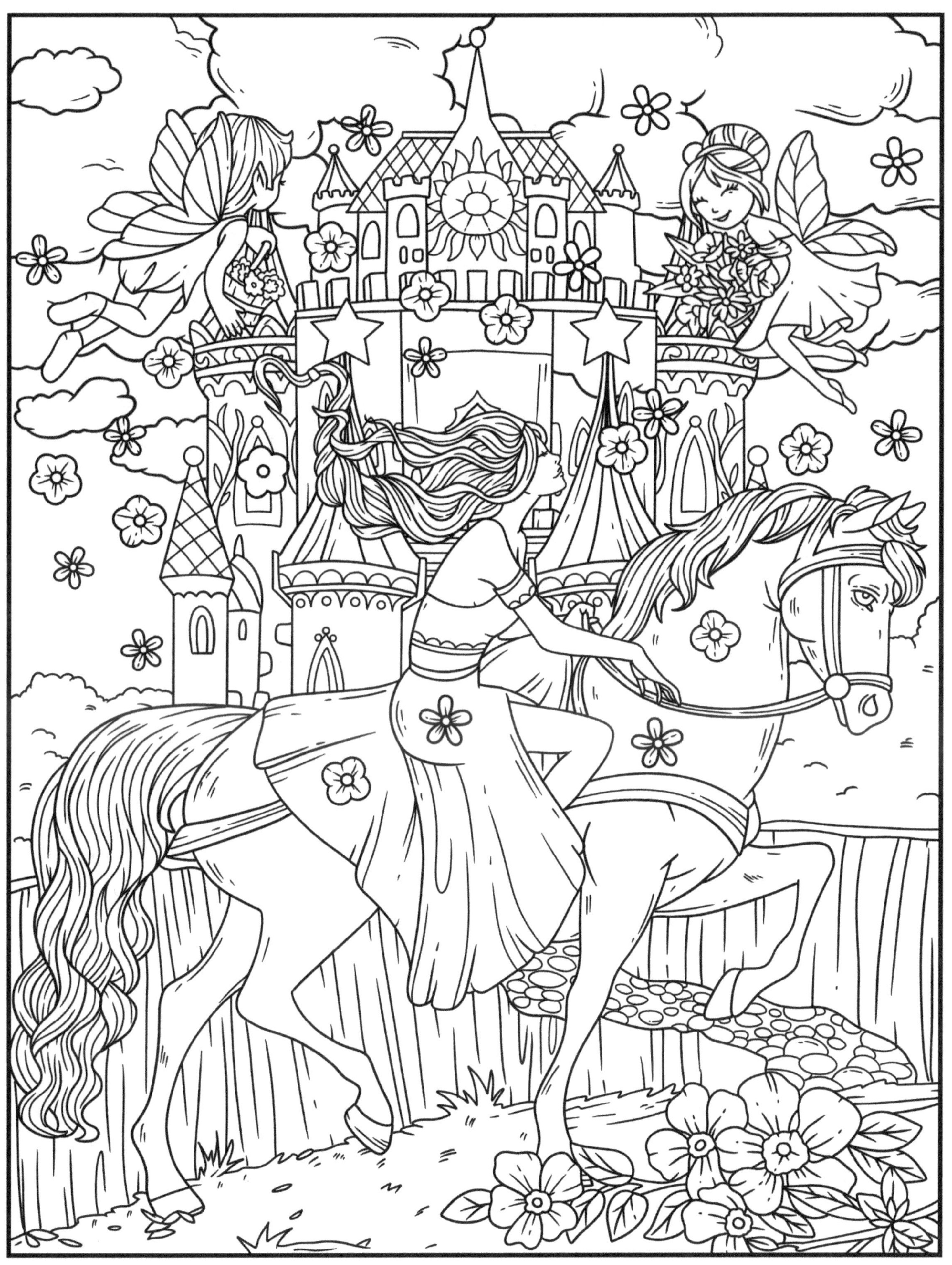

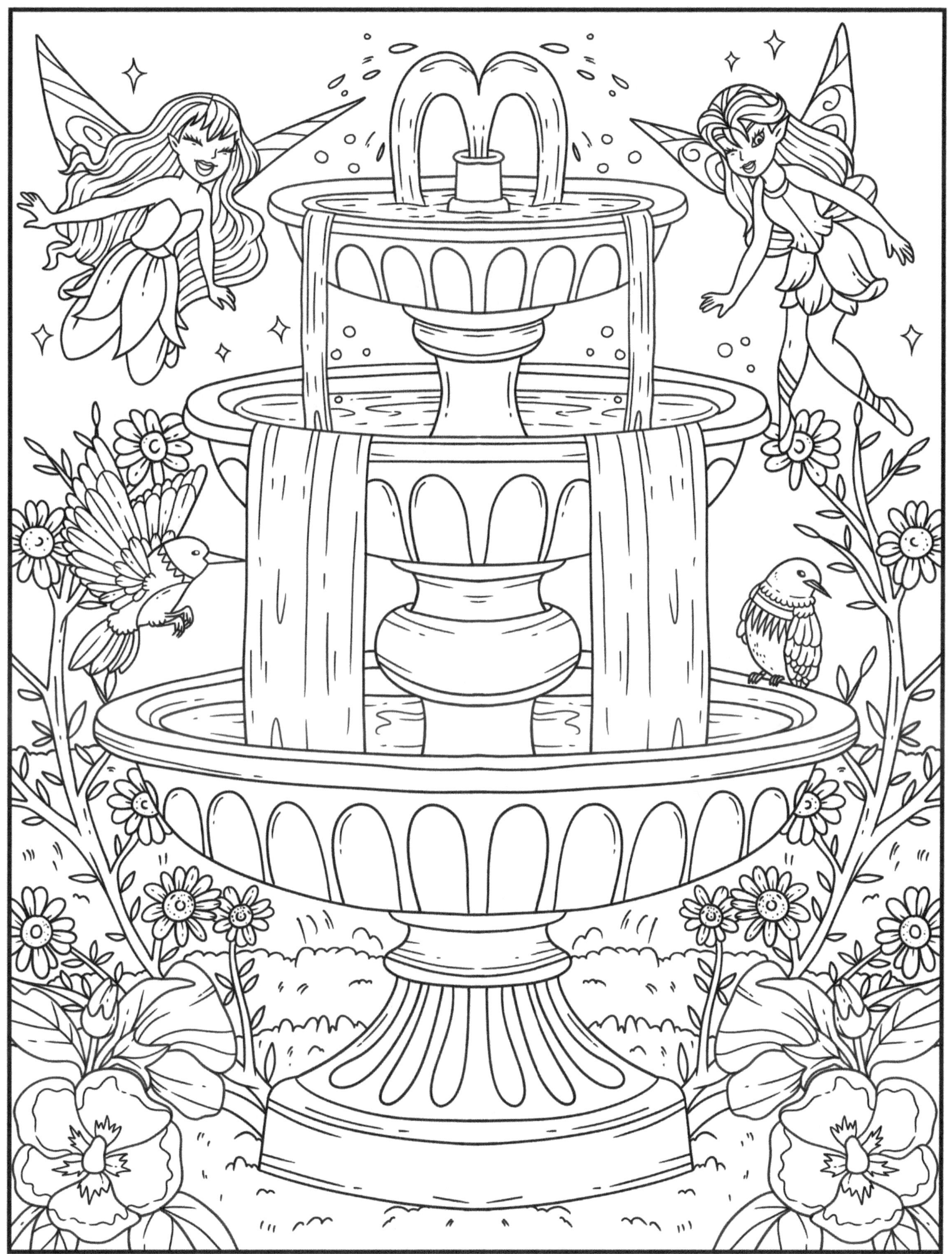

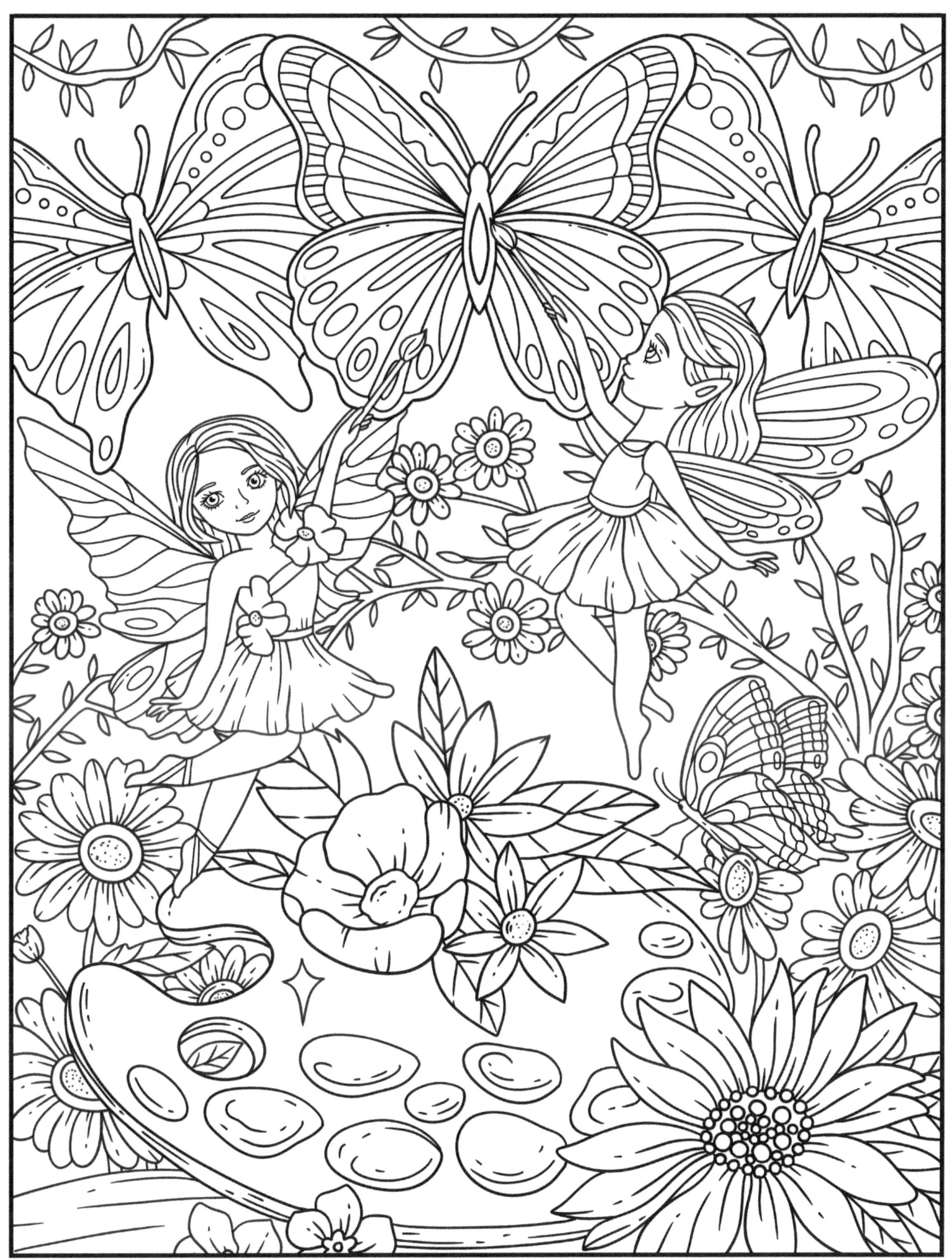

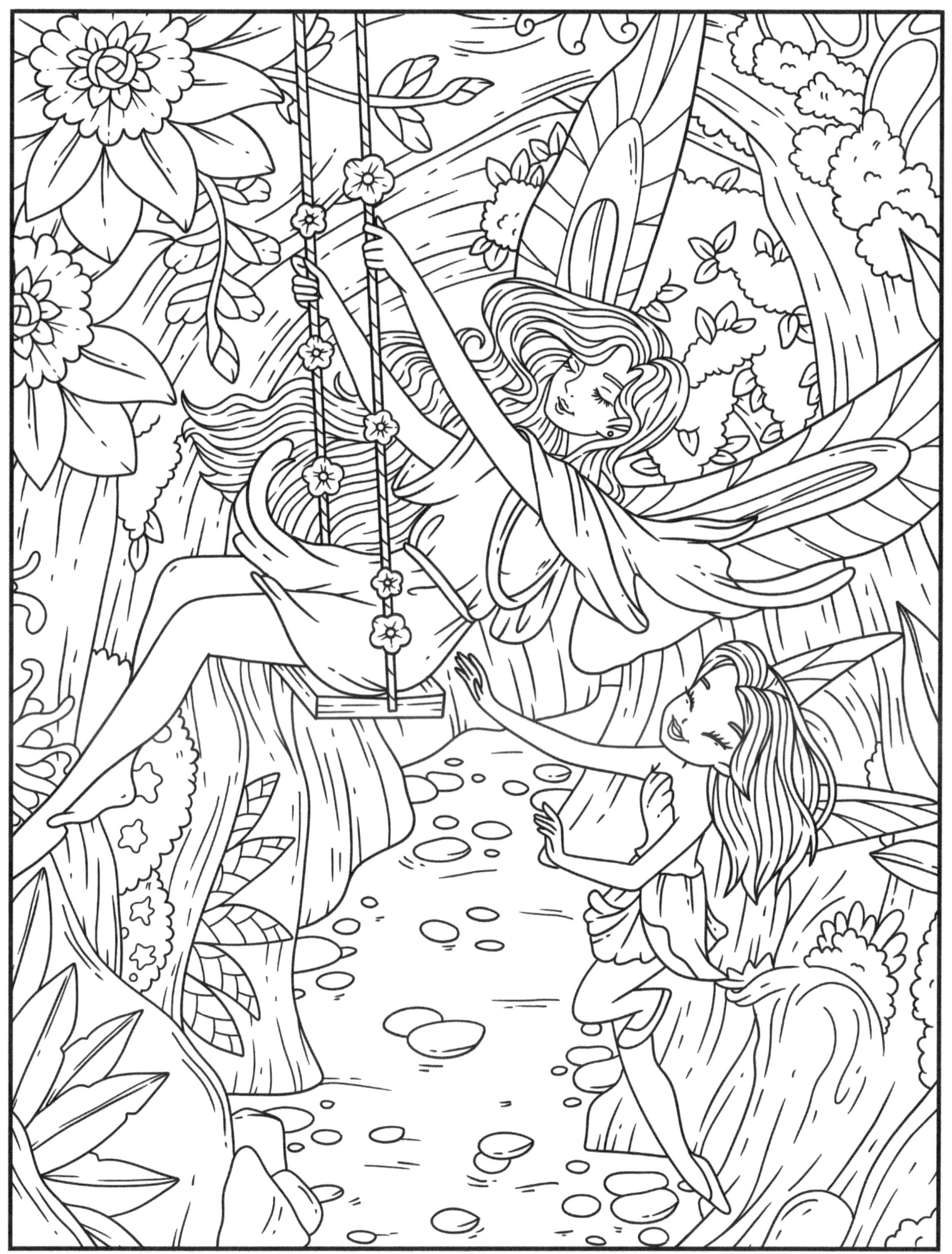

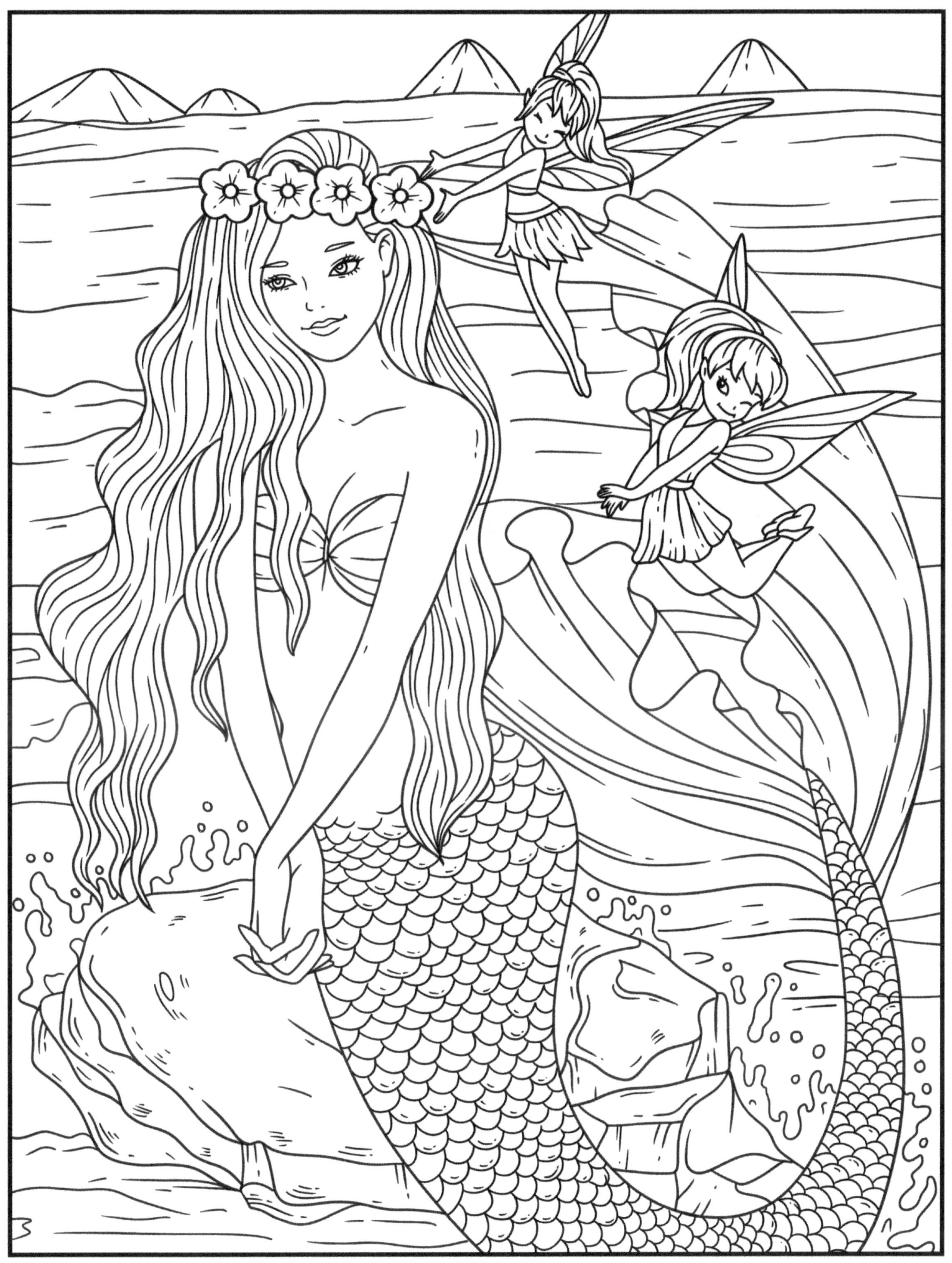

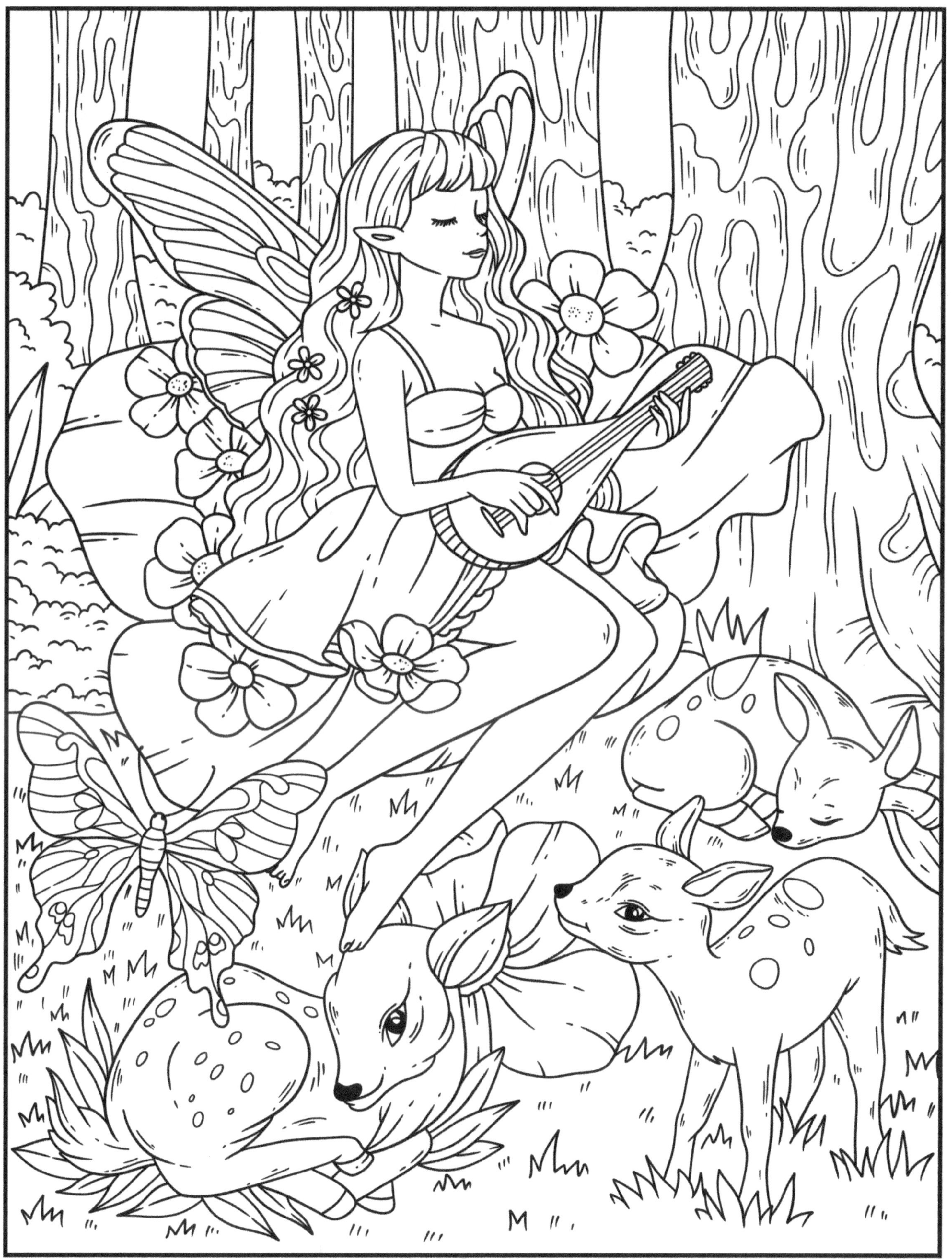

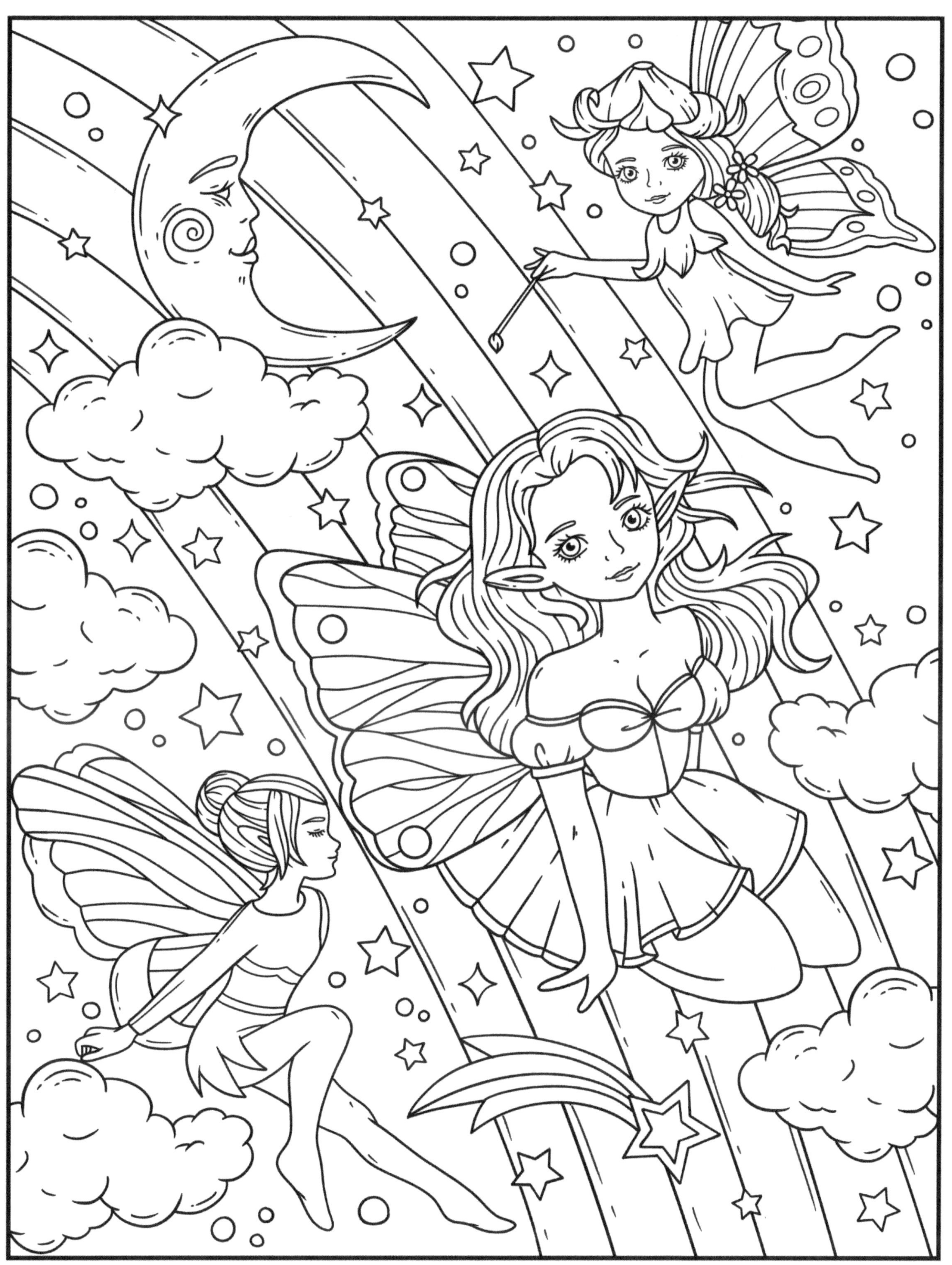

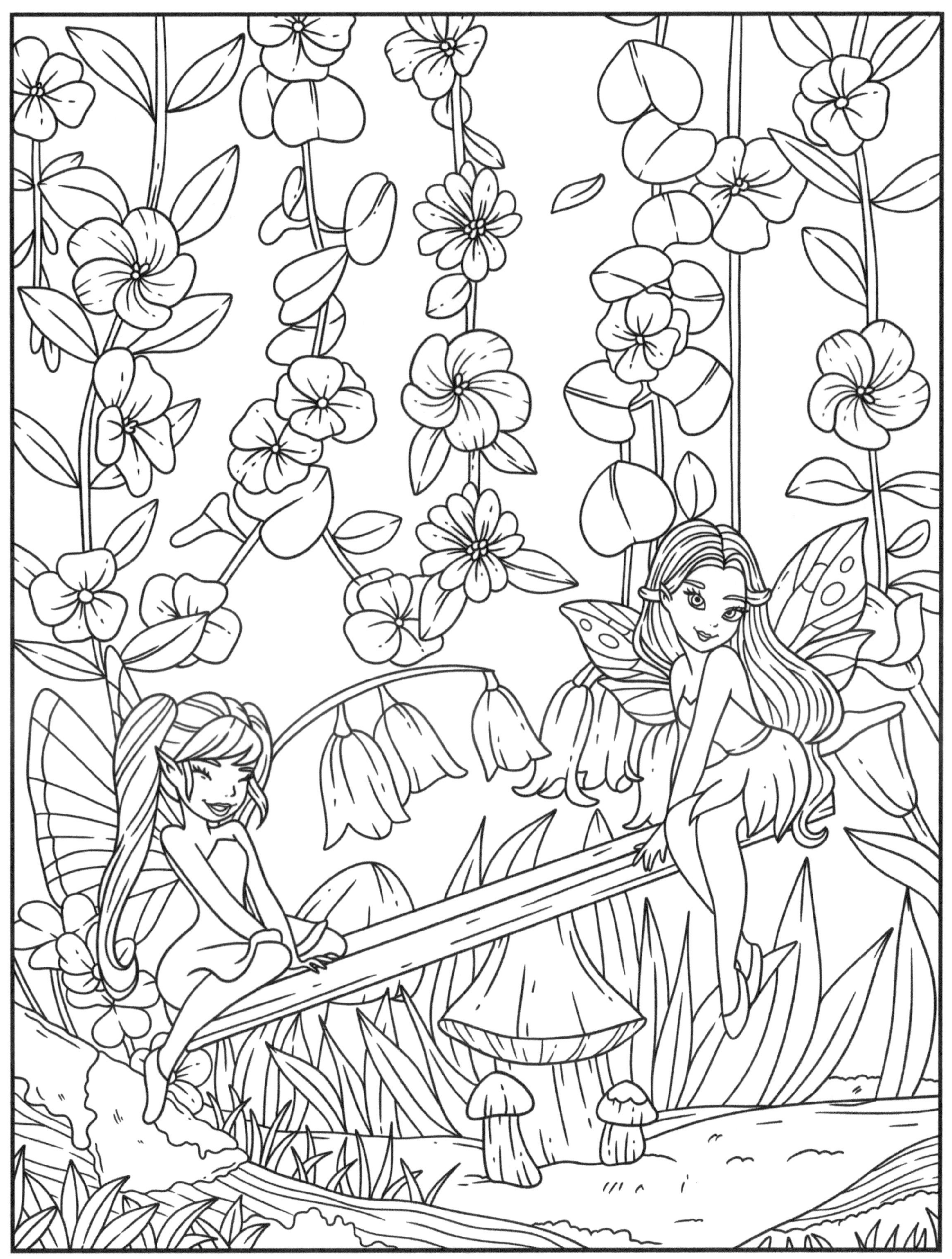

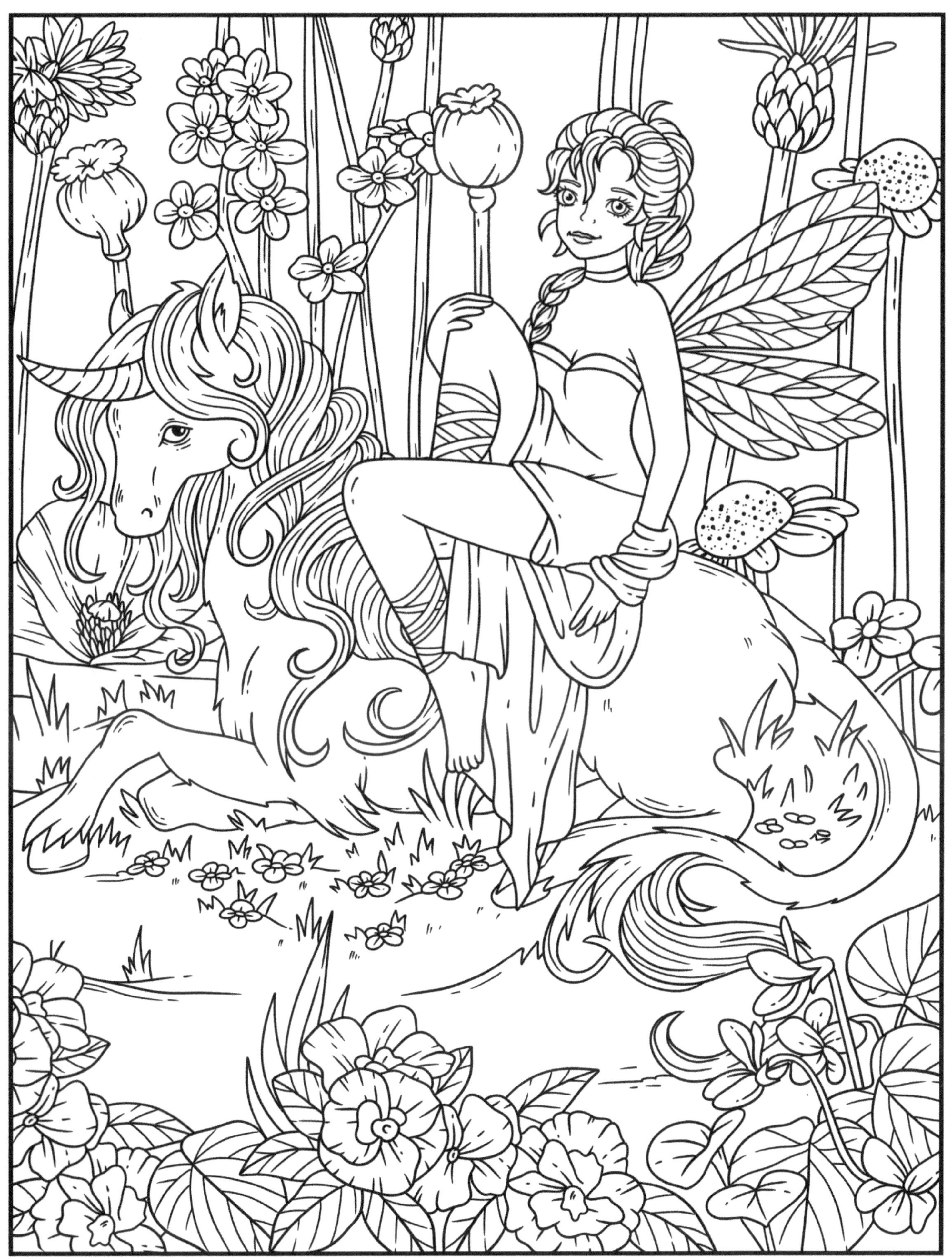

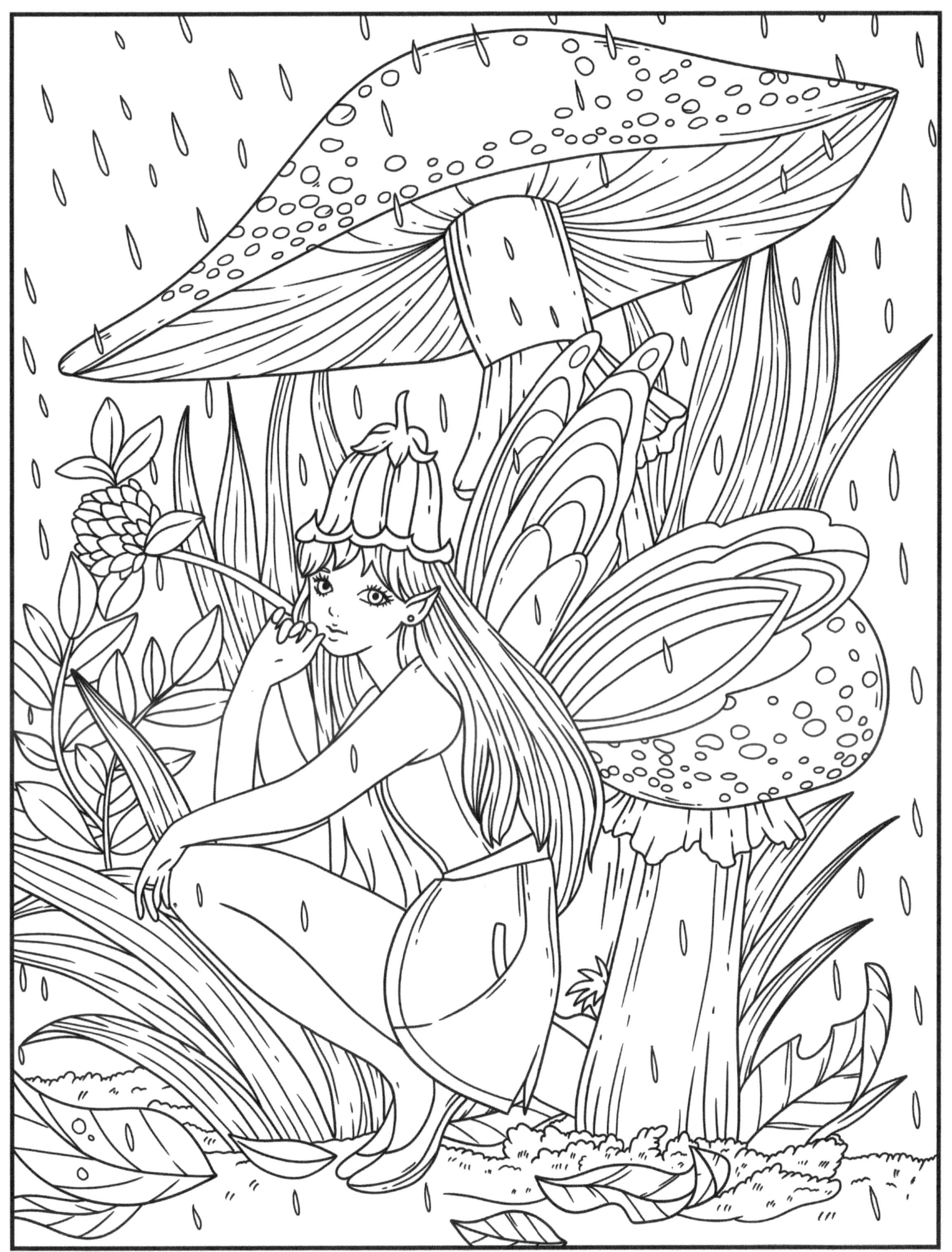

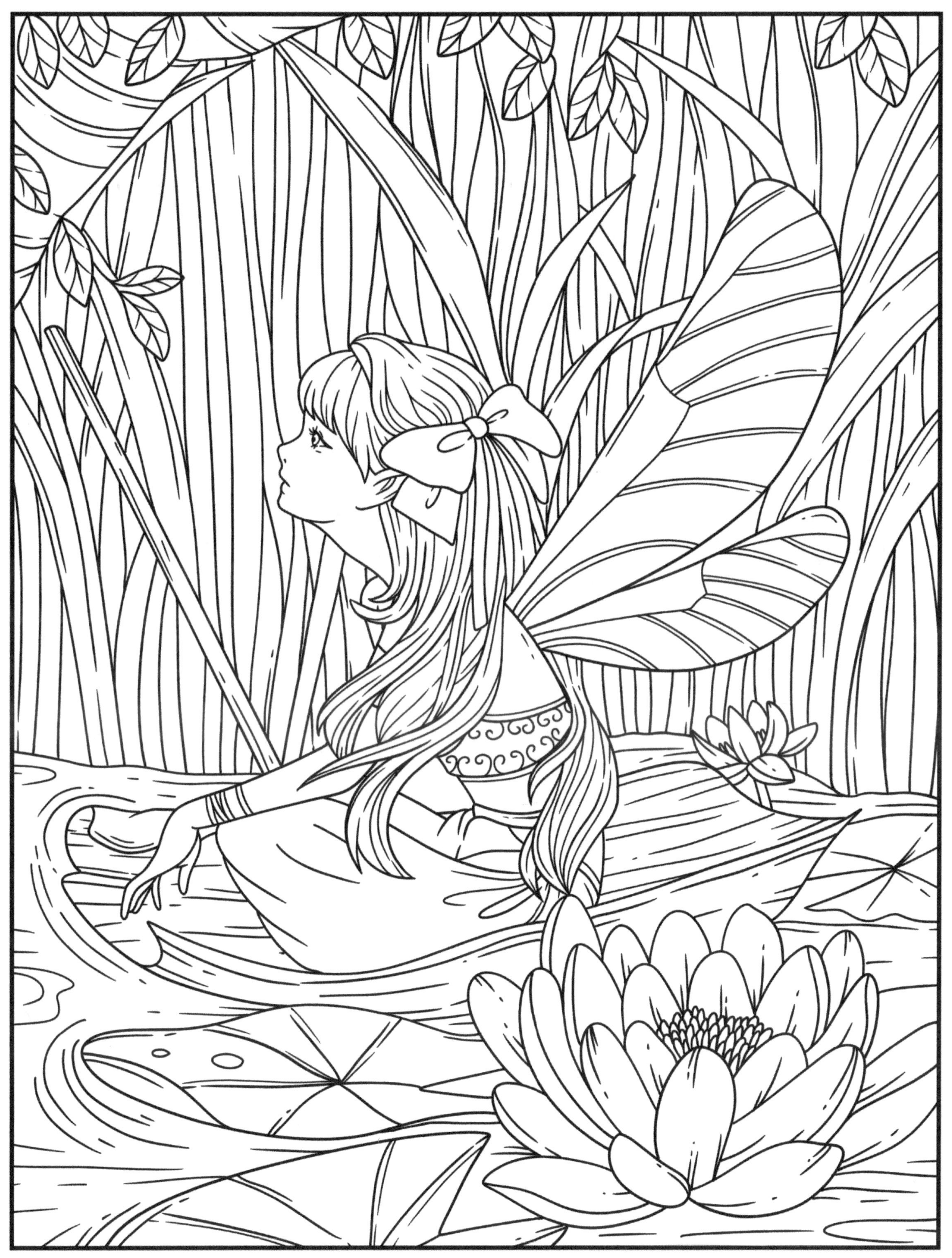